T0244689

BEYOND THE INTERNATIONALE

Revolutionary writing
by Eugène Pottier, Communard

Edited and translated by Loren Kruger

LA COMMUNE   Nº 39

POTTIER (EUGÈNE)

Eugène Pottier, songwriter. Photograph by Félix Tournachon, known as Nadar. Courtesy of the Bibliothèque Nationale de France

BEYOND THE INTERNATIONALE

Revolutionary Writing
by Eugène Pottier, Communard

Edited and translated
by
Loren Kruger

Charles H. Kerr Publishing Company
Chicago

ISBN 978-0-88286-032-9

Cover: Eugène Pottier. Caricature by Hippolyte Mailly.
Published in *La Commune* 1871.
Courtesy, Museum of the Hôtel de Ville, Paris

Subversive Literature for the Whole Family Since 1886

Charles H. Kerr Publishing Company
8901 S. Exchange Ave. #1
Chicago, IL 60617
charleshkerr.com

TABLE OF CONTENTS

Napoleon Bonaparte Statue Toppled by Communards at the Place Vendome,
Paris. April 1871. Photograph by Bruno Braquehais. Courtesy,
Bibliothèque Nationale, Paris

INTRODUCTION

Many people know the *Internationale*, the rousing anthem of solidarity for working people the world over, but few in the English-speaking realm know the history of its evolution or its author, Eugène Pottier (1816–87). Pottier penned the *Internationale* in the wake of the collapse of the short-lived but memorable Paris Commune of 1871, but he wrote many revolutionary songs and poems before and after the Commune. Some, like the *Internationale*, look forward to revolution, even when faced with temporary defeat. Others offer wry takes on more traditional lyric subjects such as the life of a child, his daughter Marguerite. Still others tackle modern and perhaps unpoetic topics as relevant in the twenty-first century as they were in the nineteenth, topics such as astronomy, ecology, or political economy. In the nineteenth century, these songs were sung in plebeian singing clubs called *goguettes* and printed first in pamphlet form. In the twentieth and twenty-first centuries, French publishers have continued to reprint Pottier's work, most recently in a bicentennial selection of *Poèmes et chansons* [Poems and Songs] in 2016, but he is unknown in the English-speaking world. Today, after both Pottier's bicentennial and the sesqui-centennial of the Commune have come and gone, it is time for the English-speaking world to read beyond the *Internationale* to the work that Pottier wrote from the revolutions of 1848 to his death in 1887.

Eugène Pottier was born shortly after the defeat of Napoleon and the restoration of the French monarchy in 1815. He started his working life as a packer like his father but went on to train and work as an industrial textile designer. He began to write songs and poems already at age thirteen, after the uprising of 1830 had deposed King Charles X in favor of Louis-Philippe. At the age of thirty-two, Pottier participated in the republican uprisings in February and June 1848 as a writer of revolutionary songs, which he performed in partnership with singer-songwriter Gustave Nadaud (1820–93). Even after Louis-Napoleon Bonaparte's coup d'état and his rule of the Second Empire as Napoleon III (1851–70), Pottier continued to write poetry critical of the regime. By the time that the Paris Commune was proclaimed in March 1871, Pottier was a seasoned activist affiliated with the First International Working Men's Association (IWMA) founded in 1864 by Karl Marx together with local and émigré socialists in London and was one of several older Communards who could compare 1871 with 1848. Elected to represent the second *arrondissement* [district] of Paris after the restoration of the republic in 1870, in the first city council to organize delegates under the new arrondissement system established in 1867, he later served in the eleventh during the Commune. Pottier co-authored several Commune documents, including the Artists' Manifesto headed by painter Gustave Courbet.

Although the legend persists that the *Internationale* was performed on the barricades as the Commune faced the final battle with the French army in May 1871, Pottier wrote the words *after* the fall of the Commune in Paris, as Pierre Brochon indicates in his notes to Pottier's *Oeuvres complètes*, before he fled via Belgium to England and later to the United States. Published as a pamphlet only after the Third French Republic granted amnesty to Communards and thus reentry to Pottier and his comrades in 1880, as Marc Ferro notes, the *Internationale* was initially accompanied by the familiar tune of *La Marseillaise*, the French republican anthem from 1793, which was still listed as the accompaniment when the song was published in Pottier's *Chants révolutionnaires* in April 1887. The new—and today definitive—score by Pierre Degeyter (1848–1932) had its first outing in 1888, after Pottier's death, at the *Lyre des Travailleurs*, a workers' song contest in the northern industrial city of Lille. It reached an international audience with the U.S. translation in 1894 by Charles H. Kerr, whose publishing house in Chicago had been active since 1886. The first German translation, by Emil Luckhardt in 1896, was produced at the urging of German Socialist Party leader Wilhelm Liebknecht who had heard the original sung at the congress of the *Parti ouvrier* [French Workers Party; est. 1882] in Lille in 1894. In the century and a quarter since that congress, the *Internationale* has circulated in more than eighty languages or dialects, among them two U.S. versions, a nineteenth-century English translation, and an updated adaptation by Billy Bragg, which he wrote in 1990 to affirm that the *Internationale* could and should "unite the world in song" in the post-Cold War era. In its many versions, the *Internationale* is still the foremost anthem of struggles for social justice and equality worldwide—but its author and his contribution to the Paris Commune have been largely forgotten.

After only seventy-two days of debate, innovation, and struggle, the Paris Commune of 1871—capitalized to highlight its singular influence—went down in flames during the so-called Bloody Week of reprisals by the French army, in which up to thirty thousand Communards and bystanders died. Pottier was able to escape the slaughter—by fleeing to England and then to the United States, where he lived until 1880. While in the U.S., he wrote more poems and songs, as well as speeches that he gave to gatherings of fellow socialists and freemasons, whether French exiles or U.S. allies, in New York, New Jersey, and Boston, which were printed for circulation by socialists as far away as San Francisco. After the Third Republic granted amnesty to surviving Communards in 1880, Pottier returned to Paris. He was by then suffering from partial paralysis but he nonetheless entered the workers' song competition *La Lice Chansonnière* [Singers' Platform] in 1883, when it was presided over by former Communards such as Jules Vallès (1832–88), author of the Communard novel *L'Insurgé*, and Pottier's collaborator Nadaud, who had sung his ballads since 1848. Pottier's song *Chacun vit de son métier* [To Each His Trade] won the silver medal. It was published along with others by Pottier and his comrades in chapbooks costing a few centimes a piece, and in 1884, a small collection with a grand title—*Poésies d'économie sociale et chants socialistes révoluionnaires* [Social Economic Poems and Revolutionary Socialist Songs]—featured more of his poems. These and many others, including the *Internationale*, were assembled by a Communard poet turned editor, Jean Allemane, under the title *Chants révolutionnaires* [Revolutionary Songs] and published in April 1887 with appreciative prefaces by Allemanne, Nadaud, and Vallès to raise funds for their ailing comrade.

When Pottier died in November 1887, his songs were popular enough to inspire ten thousand people to follow his funeral cortège. According to eyewitness Ernest Museux, mourners at Père Lachaise Cemetery in the proletarian twentieth arrondissement in the east of Paris rallied behind the Commune's red flag even after the police threatened to take the flag away. Among those ten thousand were Communards such as Allemanne, Nadaud, and Vallès, as well as the teacher and writer Louise Michel, and Paul Lafargue, Marx's son-in-law. This outpouring of support expressed not only mourning for one Communard, but ongoing commitment to the Commune's project of social revolution. The next section sketches the key points of this revolutionary experiment, which resonated the world over thanks to the telegraph and the trans-Atlantic cable that had been laid in 1867, as Quentin Deluermoz notes, a few years before the Commune.

The Commune of 1871 and its Legacy

Although the Commune survived only seventy-two days from March 18 to May 28, 1871, its proposals to transform social, economic, and cultural life in Paris still resonate worldwide more than a hundred and fifty years later. Although these proposals could not be fully realized, they influenced Third Republic France in the decades thereafter and inspired revolutionaries around the world, from Vladimir Ilyich Ulyanov, a.k.a. Lenin, to anarchists as well as socialists in the U.S. The actions that led to the declaration of an independent Commune began when Parisians rose against the Prussians who had defeated France in the 1870 war fomented by Louis Bonaparte. Bonaparte was forced to abdicate in favor of a new conservative republican government after the Prussian siege of Paris in September and the threat of more radical republican rebellion in the communes, in the everyday sense of municipal governments, in Lyon and Marseilles as well as Paris. When the national government finally capitulated to Prussia in January 1871, Parisians resisted government attempts to subdue the city. When soldiers tried on March 18 to disarm the popular National Guards and confiscate the cannon that had been purchased by public subscription to defend the city, Parisians blocked their way and moved the cannon to higher ground, notably to Montmartre. Prime minister Adolphe Thiers and his government responded to this defiance and to the fraternization between Parisian National Guards and government troops by summoning the National Assembly and the troops to Versailles, the palace that had housed the kings of France. Eight days later, on March 26, Parisians elected an autonomous city government, and the Commune was officially proclaimed on March 28.

The Internationalists among the Communards were inspired more by the project of forging egalitarian labor relations such as the workshops that had animated the uprisings in 1848 and the program of the IWMA since 1864, than by revolutionary terror on the model of 1793 that inspired Lenin, even if their Jacobin and Blanquist rivals argued that the harsh suppression of dissent was necessary to maintain a united front in the military and ideological battle against Versailles. The Commune created workers' cooperatives in factories abandoned by owners who had fled Paris during the siege, mandated a minimum wage and fair compensation for elected officials to discourage bribery, and abolished pawnshop debts. In the sphere of equal rights, the Commune recognized the pivotal role of women, starting, as Carolyn Eichner demonstrates, with those who had stood between the cannon and soldiers who were trying to confiscate them. The Commune attempted to fund education and care for all children, whether their parents were married in church or not, in recognition that unmarried working mothers were at the forefront of the defense of Paris. In the sphere of education, the Commune established schools for girls and boys, progressive secular instruction above all by women who received pay equal to male teachers. The Commune embraced as citizens foreign-born members of the International, such as Léo Fraenkel from Austro-Hungarian Budapest (1844–96) or Elisabeth Dmitrieff (1850–1917) from St. Petersburg, Russia, who had demonstrated their commitment to the Commune. In the sphere of politics, the Commune encouraged free debate among many competing factions of socialists, anarchists, proponents of autonomous workers' cooperatives as against those proposing nationalization of the Bank of France, a move which, in Marx's view, could have fortified the Commune by preventing the bank from sending funds to Versailles. And, in the sphere of culture, Courbet, Pottier, and others writing the Artists' Manifesto encouraged Parisian artisans as well as self-taught artists to express themselves and to contribute to public art in the city.

After the amnesty of 1880, the National Assembly recognized the republic's revolutionary heritage by adding key dates such as July 14, the day in 1789 on which Parisians stormed the Bastille, to the official calendar. Socialist and worker parties, as well as moderate republicans committed to social improvements, passed legislation securing fairer wages for workers, women as well as men, the liberalization of divorce, and government funding for health care, including childcare, as well as education (Mayeux). While this legislation granted social and economic benefits to workers and their children, the Workers Party, to which feminist Communards such as Paule Mink (1839–1901), the French daughter of Polish immigrants, belonged, focused on social equality rather than voting rights for women, who gained the franchise only in 1944, after General De Gaulle proclaimed France liberated from Nazi occupation. Nor did the Third Republic follow up on the Commune's radical extension of citizenship to international activists. Birthright citizenship for children born in France was enacted in the 1880s but unevenly extended to European migrants, let alone people of color from French colonies. Although the government granted amnesty to Communards and appropriated some of their egalitarian proposals, the police continued surveillance of individual Communards. Louise Michel (1830–1905) returned to France after enforced exile in the colony of New Caledonia but her advocacy on behalf of bakery and other workers landed her in a French prison, and when renewed activism after her release prompted the state to try to commit her to a mental asylum, she fled to London (Michel, *Red Virgin*). On May 1, 1901, thirty years after the Commune, Paule Mink's funeral drew thousands of mourners singing the *Internationale* despite police officers lining the route (Eichner, *Surmounting the Barricades*). And, in March 1921, on the fiftieth anniversary, the French Communist Party (est. 1920) organized marches to commemorate the Commune; the Communist newspaper reported both on these commemorations and on the government's attempt to stop them (*L'Humanité*).

The upheavals of the 1960s, from the battle for Algerian independence which concluded in 1962 to the student and worker revolt in 1968, encouraged more interest in the Commune in France. Arthur Adamov's sprawling pageant *Le printemps de 71* (1961), which featured fictional as well as historical actors from the Commune, Henri Lefebvre's study *La Proclamation de la Commune* (The Proclamation of the Commune, 1965), and the publication of Pottier's *Oeuvres completes* (Collected Works, 1966) preceded the centenary. In 1971, André Benedetto's *Commune de Paris*, a chronicle by performers representing historical individuals as well as voices in chorus, while pulling a facsimile cannon and holding aloft the emblematic red flag, played out on the streets of Avignon during the annual festival in August. The centenary also prompted two long-playing records featuring L'*Internationale* and *Le Temps des Cérises* [Cherry Time, by Jean-Baptiste Clément], alongside less familiar songs from the era. More recent publications include a collection of photographs from the Musée D'Orsay (Bajac 2000). Historian Jacques Rougerie published his first book on the Commune in 1971 and became its premier historian until his death, almost on its anniversary, on March 22, 2022. And in 2016, demonstrators in the nationwide *Nuit debout* [night on the march] movement against President Emmanuel Macron's attempt to curtail pensions, raise the retirement age, and enact restrictions on labor rights temporarily renamed the Place de la République in central Paris, the Place de la Commune (Deluermoz).

In contrast with the legitimation in France of the Commune as an important part of European history, as well as a key event in the evolution of international movements for justice and equality, the reception of the Commune in the U.S. has been more fragmented. In the aftermath of Bloody Week at the end of May 1871, establishment figures such as Elihu Washburn, U.S. ambassador to France from 1869 to 1887, dismissed the Commune as a pernicious example of anarchist troublemaking, as Philip Katz recounts, prompting Pottier to lambast Washburn in his speech honoring the Commune in New Jersey in 1878. (See Part One below.) Despite the disdain expressed by Washburn and his ilk, the Commune's model of social equality, shared with U.S. allies by Communards in exile such as the geographer Elisée Reclus as well as Pottier, inspired social revolutionists—to use the term of the times—across the U.S. from the East to the West Coast and up and down the Midwest from Wisconsin to Missouri via Chicago, as Bruce Nelson shows.

In Chicago in particular, the International Working Peoples Association (IWPA), led by native-born Americans Albert Parsons and his wife Lucy Parsons in cooperation with immigrants from Europe, especially Germany, such as August Spies, organized yearly commemorative rallies on March 18, including at least one on the Chicago lakefront in 1877, which, according to police estimates, drew at least forty thousand people to events that included picnics, choral singing, gymnastic competitions, and theatre (Nelson; Kruger, "Cold Chicago"). On May 4, 1886, at the end of an IWPA demonstration in support of a strike against McCormick Reaper Company, an unexplained bomb in Haymarket Square provoked a police riot, a trial that swept up Parsons, Spies, and others who had left the event before the bomb dropped, and, the next year, the execution of these leaders. (For this history, see: Avrich, Green, and Roediger/Rosemont.) Pottier was aware of commemorations of the Commune during his time in the U.S. from 1873 to 1880. Several poems from this period, especially *The Workingmen of America to the Workingmen of France* (1876) and *The Commune Came Through Here* (1879), emphasize the affinities between American and French socialists. Although Pottier does not mention the Haymarket incident, he wrote his most emphatic commemorative poem *The Commune Did Not Die* in May 1886, after telegraph news of the bomb on Haymarket Square and the police reprisals had reached Europe, and his colleague Jules Jouy wrote a song commemorating the [Haymarket] martyrs after their execution in 1887 (Brécy "A propos").

Although the IWPA and later the Industrial Workers of the World (IWW; founded 1905) continued to commemorate the Commune in the U.S., police repression of alleged opponents of the U.S. entry into World War I led to mass arrests. The government continued to suppress dissent after the war with the so-called Palmer Raids ordered in 1919 by Attorney General Mitchell Palmer and implemented by the then-new Bureau of Investigation (now the FBI). Despite this crackdown, the Commune was not forgotten in the Americas. On May 1, Workers' Day, 1921, roughly the fiftieth anniversary of the Commune, the IWW paper *The Industrial Worker* published a sketch of marchers carrying signs in several languages; although the sketch does not name the Commune, the sign in French—*Prolétaires de tous les pays, unissez-vous!*—was the second most prominent banner after the English *Workers of the World Unite!* (Roediger/Rosemont), reflecting not only the final words of *The Communist*

Manifesto but also the core message of the *Internationale*. The Commune's worldwide appeal also resonated in fiftieth anniversary commemorations in 1937 of the Haymarket executions in 1887 documented for instance in Uruguay, as well as in New York and Chicago.

In the twenty-first century, the Commune and the Haymarket have inspired commemorations and revisions. In May 2011, Pocket Guide to Hell Tours, a revisionist reenactment company (2008–2015) organized a 125th anniversary reenactment of the Haymarket strike, protest, and subsequent trial on site in Chicago (Kruger, "What Time is this Place?"). In the spring of 2012, the "public rehearsal" of *Days of the Commune*, Bertolt Brecht's 1949 play about the 1871 Commune, directed by Zoë Beloff on New York City streets and sites that had been temporarily held by the Occupy Movement in the autumn of 2011, followed the arc of the Commune by performing one or two scenes every weekend from March 18 to the end of May (Beloff; Kruger, "Performance, Politics, and Historiography"). Occupy Movement participants also alluded to the Commune in retrospective accounts (Khatib et al) and, as Enzo Traverso noted in *Jacobin* magazine on the Commune's 150th anniversary, even without explicit references, the Occupy Movement resembled the Commune in several ways, from the participation of precarious intellectuals and informal workers to decentered governance. The actions of its successor movements, such as the Debt Collective, recall the Commune's attack on debt as an instrument of oppression.

The Paris Commune of 1871 has generated historical analysis in many languages and, as the brief account above suggests, also left informal traces, but writing by the Communards themselves has been translated only fitfully into English. Prosper-Olivier Lissagaray's *History of the Commune* (1877), in the nineteenth-century translation by Eleanor Marx, is no longer in print; neither is *The Red Virgin*, Louise Michel's memoir. Among those Communards who spent time in the U.S., Reclus wrote essays on anarchy, geography, and modernity which have been published in English by PM, a small press in Oakland, California. Pottier's *Chants révoluionnaires* came out before his death in 1887, and his work was reprinted several times before World War I—but not much in English, apart from the *Internationale*. Several texts by Pottier appeared in the Soviet Union in anthologies in Russian and in German devoted to the Commune, and in other languages such as Turkish, even before Pottier's *Collected Works* were published by the then pre-eminent French leftist press Éditions Maspero in 1966, one hundred and fifty years after Pottier's birth. Le Temps des cérises, the press named after Clément's popular song, commemorated the bicentennial of Pottier's birth in 2016 with a selection of his poems and songs. In contrast, only a few short pieces have appeared in English translation: one poem "Don Quixote" in a U.S. collection of anti-clerical poems called *The Atheist's Prayer*, and informal translations of six of Pottier's poems by Mitchell Abidor on the website: www.marxists.org. *The Communards*, Abidor's translated collection of Communard speeches and documents, accompanied by short biographies of some participants, is useful but, although Pottier was among the named authors listed on several Commune declarations, he does not appear in Abidor's book. Nor do any of the many women active in the Commune. (See Godineau and Rey in French and Eichner in English.)

The Shape of this Book

Beyond the International aims to give Pottier the attention that he deserves in the English language and to highlight for an international audience the diversity of his writing. What is remarkable is his range across genres and his attention to modern questions such as the use and abuse of science in society as well as to the persistent problems of social inequality. Part One uses Pottier's own words to introduce the author. This section begins with two letters in which he recalls his life and formation as a worker and a writer, before turning to speeches that he made to honor the Commune and those who continued to fight for social justice. These speeches were delivered during his U.S. exile from 1875 to 1880 to gatherings of French comrades-in-exile and U.S. allies in local organizations, such as the Socialist Labor Party whose *Labor News* published a translation of the *International* in 1911, and in the local lodges of the transnational freemason network. Although Pottier does not discuss the history of the freemasons, he was aware of their contribution to free-thinking in the eighteenth-century Enlightenment and the Revolution of 1789, and to the anti-clerical sentiment that influenced the insurgents of 1848 and 1871, even if some freemasons such as the Protestant François Guizot (1787–1874) were more conservative. The New York lodge *Les Égalitaires* [The Egalitarians] to which Pottier applied in 1875, was founded by French socialist exiles who would later support the firm separation of church and state enacted by the Third Republic.

Pottier's speeches are often quite lyrical, even when he is emphatically defending the Commune. Their rhythm, especially in the eulogy that he gave in March 1878 to commemorate the Communard dead "buried in such haste that they lay dying, barely covered with the earth that fell into their ditches" echoes the cadences of poetry as well as the rhetorical emphases of oratory designed to rouse his audience to action. Conversely, many poems and songs, while lyrical in form, wax downright angry over exploitation inflicted on working people by the ruling classes and, in contrast, offer soberly analytical attempts to examine the hidden workings of capital.

Part Two forms the heart of the book with thirty-three poems and songs selected from more than six hundred in his collected works. The poems that I have translated span several decades from 1848 to 1887 and reveal Pottier's mastery of classical forms such as the sonnet as well as the plebeian and often overtly political songs (*chansons*), which show off his ability to make poetry and song out of plebeian language. Many songs, such as *Johnny Misery* celebrate working people and criticize the persistence of drudgery and inequality in the Third Republic. Some commemorate the Commune, such as *The Commune came through here* (1878), while others express personal attachments such as the poem about his daughter Marguerite. In addition to more traditional lyric poems, Pottier also wrote texts that are shaped like poems but which analyze key political and economic concepts. For instance, *Estates General* and *Liberty, Equality, Fraternity* (both 1848) critique the bourgeois revolution of 1789 and celebrate the broader aspirations of 1848, while *Political Economy* (1881), dedicated with irony to the professors of the Collège de France who rationalized the laissez-faire economic policy that impoverished ordinary people, argued that the Third Republic exacerbated rather than mitigated the inequality that had provoked the uprisings of 1848 and 1871. Pottier emphasized this fusion of poetry and political analysis in the title of his collection *Social Economic Poems and Revolutionary Socialist Songs* (1884), which brought together many of the above poems, which were originally published in cheap pamphlets to facilitate circulation and public singing.

Some poems, such as *The New Era* or *The Exposition* (on the Exposition of Industrial Arts in Paris in 1861), highlight Pottier's expertise as an industrial designer alongside a pervasive faith in workers' mastery of industrial progress which animates many nineteenth-century socialist texts, most famously *The Communist Manifesto*. Others treat scientific discoveries with wonder but also with skeptical regard, on the grounds that science has yet to solve social problems such as inequality and outright hunger, for instance *Newton's Apple* (1849) or *The Phases of Equality* (1878). The longest poem in this book, to which Pottier gave the English title *The Workingmen of America to the Workingmen of France* (1876) even though he wrote the poem itself in French, challenges the enthusiastic observer of *The Exposition*—perhaps Pottier's younger self—with an indictment of the rapaciousness of American capitalism, presented as though by U.S. workers welcoming French newcomers to the Centennial Exposition in Philadelphia in 1876. Although the brisk introduction to the poem offers a *welcome* in English from workers to workers in the spirit of international solidarity, the six parts that follow in more complex stanzas analyze both the spectacular allure of the world exposition that had captivated Pottier in Second Empire Paris and the darker side of the exploitation that fueled the rise of the U.S.

In addition to translations of Pottier's poems, songs, ballads, and speeches that English-speaking readers are less likely to know, *Beyond the Internationale* includes the *Internationale* in several languages. Part Three includes, in addition to *L'Internationale* in original French, several English and U.S. versions whose translators from Charles H. Kerr (1894) to Billy Bragg (1990) are well known. Since most but not all versions in English were written in rhyme for choral delivery, individual verses vary considerably, even if most use Degeyter's score. The several versions of the anthem in English highlight differences even between the roughly contemporary nineteenth century English and U.S. texts, and still more between these militant calls to join in battle for the "final conflict" and Bragg's ecumenical chorus a century later—"So come brothers and sisters/For the struggle carries on/The *Internationale*/ Unites the world in song"—which he wrote in response to a call by Pete Seeger to revive international solidarity in 1990 when the end of the Cold War prompted some pundits to proclaim the end of history and thus the end of the struggle for justice and equality.

Part Four assembles adaptations of the *Internationale* in languages from Afrikaans to Zulu, by way of Catalan, Dutch, Galician, Italian, Portuguese, Russian, and Yiddish, as well as two German and six Spanish versions. I have included the names of translators where available, but readers should note that many versions of the *Internationale* circulate in audio recordings without attribution to an individual. The adaptations included in this book represent a small sample of the eighty-plus recordings in circulation.

Translation Practices

Moving between different occasions for reading or performance demands flexible attention to form and function and thus calls for flexible translation practices rather than a single translation philosophy. If I were to avow an overarching method, it would be to focus on translating the meaning of the *whole text or utterance*—the poem, the song, or the speech—and the intended function of that utterance rather than looking for equivalents for a single word or line, a habit that ends up distorting the sense of the whole. My translations of Pottier's prose and poetry in Parts One and Two attempt to capture the nineteenth-century idiom of the original texts while also anticipating the occasion of their reading—or singing—by English-speakers in the twenty-first century. Marching songs favor rhyming lines and a forward-driving rhythm that may require adaptation to English syntax and vocabulary, and to maintain marching rhythm may depart from word-by-word equivalences, which would make the lines and the entire song clumsy and unworkable in English. On the other hand, elegies for comrades, which were intended to be read quietly, may be rendered effectively in free verse. Apart from marching songs, satires, and elegies, Pottier deployed classic lyric forms such as the sonnet, which I have rendered as sonnets in English. Speeches and letters in prose may include brief glosses on people or issues of the day that Pottier appears to assume that his audience knows but which the present-day audience likely will not.

Part Four, on the other hand, presents adaptations of the *Internationale* which have for the most part been disseminated in oral or recorded form without an identifiable translator. These versions adapt the *Internationale* to local linguistic variations of a world language—for instance, Castilian as against Latin American Spanish—or to ideological differences—for instance, communist vs. anarchist versions in Castilian Spanish. Although the Commune had an immediate albeit transient impact on participants in the brief First Spanish Republic of 1873, as Albert García-Balañà shows, the *Internationale* did not reach a wider audience in Spain until the Second Republic (1931–39). In contrast to the competing Castilian versions, the differences between the two German translations does not play out on ideological lines. The first version by Emil Luckhardt (1896) emerged initially under the auspices of the German Socialist Party (SPD) and the Second Socialist International but it was also adopted by the more militant Spartakist movement led by Karl Liebknecht and Rosa Luxemburg and the Communist Party (KPD; est 1918). The second version, by Erich Weinert (1929), while endorsed by the Communist Party, the Soviet Union, and later by East Germany, is paradoxically less militant in tone, perhaps because it was deployed to support the Popular Front Against Fascism in the 1930s. The Russian version was written by Arkady Yakovlevich Kots after he attended the 1899 meeting of French and international socialist parties in Lille. His translation, published in the London-based *Listki Zhizni* [Leaflets from Life, 1902], appears also to have influenced the imagery in the Yiddish version. The traces of Russian in the Yiddish version is not surprising because Russian was the language of secondary education for Yiddish-speakers in the Tsarist empire. Kots's version formed the basis of the Soviet anthem in 1918 but, according to Ferro, the latter changed the original's representation of the socialist future to the present tense to signal the Soviet Union's claim to represent the socialist present.

My translations of these adaptations are themselves adaptations insofar as they attempt to convey the contexts that these versions address as well as the idiom and images that they deploy. Moving out from regional particularities and ideological commitments, my reading and representations of these adaptations prompts questions about the character of their transmission, which has often been informal, if not always oral. Do the apparently anonymous adaptations reflect the style of an author yet unidentified? Or the ideological commitment of a collective, whether an organized political party or a more informal group? These questions remain unanswered for the moment but, in response to the collective character of the *Internationale*'s dissemination on a truly international scale, I have searched in every case for an idiomatic register that can convey the ideological tenor of each version while also capturing the impulse toward global solidarity that shapes all of them. I have crafted the translations in the spirit of this solidarity and trust that readers will find in this collection many connections to past and present revolutionary song.

Loren Kruger, Chicago 2024

References and Further Reading

The authors and titles below refer to texts and recording cited in the Introduction, as well as to other primary sources and recent commentary which readers should consult for further information. In cases above where I cite more than one piece by any one author, I have included an abbreviated title.

Texts by Pottier

Pottier, Eugène. *Poésies d'économie sociale et chants révolutionnaires*. Paris: Oriol, 1884.

———. *Chants révolutionnaires*. Paris: Allemane, 1887.

———. "Don Quixote." Anonymous translator. In *The Atheist's Prayer* (Berkely Heights, NJ: Oriole Press, 1934), n.p.

———. "The *Internationale*." Trans. Charles H. Kerr. *The Big Red Songbook*. Chicago: Charles H. Kerr Publishing Company, 2007.

———. *Ouvrier, Poète, Communard: Oeuvres complètes*. Ed. Pierre Brochon. Paris: Éditions Maspero, 1966.

———. *Eugène Pottier: Poèmes et chansons*. Ed. Jacques Gaucheron. Paris: Le temps des cérises, 2016.

Texts by Contemporaries

Abidor, Mitchell, ed. *The Communards: The Story of the Paris Commune by Those who Fought for It*. New York: Marxists Internet Archive Publications, 2010.

———. Translations of six songs and the *Internationale* by Eugène Pottier; https://www.marxists.org/archive/pottier/index.htm.

Lissagary, Prosper-Olivier. *Histoire de la Commune de 1871*. 1876. Paris: Éditions Maspero, 1967.

——— *History of the Commune*. Trans. Eleanor Marx. 1886. London: Verso, 2012.

Marx, Karl, and Frederick Engels. *On the Paris Commune*. New York: International Publishers, 1971.

Michel, Louise. *La Commune*. 1898. Paris: Stock, 1978.

———. *Mémoires et souvenirs*. Paris: Éditions Maspero, 1971.

_____. *The Red Virgin: Memoirs of Louise Michel.* Ed. and trans. Bullit Lowry and Elizabeth Ellington Gunter. Tuscaloosa, AL: Alabama University Press, 1981.

Museux, Ernest. *Eugène Pottier et son oeuvre.* Series: *Les défenseur du proletariat.* Paris: Allemane, 1898.

_____. *Eugène Pottier: Un défenseur du prolétariat.* Paris: Denis Editions, 2016.

Reclus, Elisée. *Anarchy, Geography, Modernity: Selected Writings.* Ed. and trans. John Clark and Camille Martin. Oakland, CA: PM Press, 2013.

Roediger, David and Franklin Rosemont, eds. *Haymarket Scrapbook* 125th anniversary edition. Chicago/Oakland: Charles H. Kerr Publishing &AK Press, 2011.

Other References

Adamov, Arthur. *Le Printemps 71.* Paris: Gallimard, 1961.

Avrich, Paul. *The Haymarket Tragedy.* Princeton: Princeton University Press, 1984.

Bajac, Quentin, et al. *La Commune photographiée.* Paris: Musée D'Orsay, 2000.

Benedetto, André. *Commune de Paris: Théâtre.* Paris: Pierre Jean Oswald, 1971.

Bensimon, Fabrice; Quentin Deluermoz, and Jeanne Monsand. Ed. *Arise Ye Wretched of the Earth: The First International in a Global Perspective.* Amsterdam: Brill, 2018.

Brécy, Robert. "A propos de «L'Internationale» d'Eugène Pottier et de Pierre Degeyter.." *Revue d'histoire moderne et contemporaine* 21,2 (1974), 300-308

Deluermoz, Quentin. *Commune(s), 1870–71: Une Traversée des mondes au XIXe siècle.* 2nd edition. Paris: Seuil, 2023.

Eichner, Carolyn. *The Paris Commune: A Brief History.* New Brunswick: Rutgers University Press, 2022.

_____*Surmounting the Barricades: Women in the Paris Commune.* Bloomington: Indiana University Press, 2004.

Ferro, Marc. *L'Internationale: Histoire d'un chant de Pottier et Degeyter.* Paris: Noésis, 1996.

García-Balañà, Albert. "1871 in Spain. Transnational and Local History in the Formation of the FRE-IWMA." In Bensimon et al, ed. *Arise Ye Wretched of the Earth*: 221–37.

Godineau, Laure. *La Commune de Paris par ceux qui l'ont vécue.* Paris: Parigramme, 2005.

Green, James. *Death in the Haymarket: A Story of Chicago, the First Labor Movement, and the Bomb That Divided Gilded Age America.* New York:

Pantheon, 2006.

Katz, Philip M. *From Appomattox to Montmartre: Americans and the Paris Commune*. Cambridge, MA: Harvard University Press, 1998.

Khatib, Kate et al. *We Are the Many: Reflections on Movement Strategy from Occupation to Liberation*. Oakland, CA: AK Press, 2012.

Kruger, Loren. "Politics, Performance and Historiography in and out of Time: American Responses to the Paris Commune," *Pamiętnik Teatralny* 70, 4 (2021), 79–101.

———. "*What Time is this Place?* Continuity, Conflict and the Right to the City: Lessons from Haymarket Square." *Performance and the Politics of Space*, 46–65. Ed Erika Fischer-Lichte and Benjamin Wihstutz. London: Routledge, 2013.

———. "Cold Chicago: Uncivil Modernity, Urban Form, and Performance in the Upstart City," TDR—*Journal of Performance Studies* 53: 3 (2009): 10–36.

Lefebvre, Henri, *La Proclamation de la Commune, 26 Mars 1871*. Paris: Gallimard, 1965.

L'Humanité. Editorial: Pour La Commune. *L'Humanité* March 21, 1921, p.1; available at: https://gallica.bnf.fr/ark:/12148/bpt6k2999788/f1.item.zoom.

Mayeur, Jean-Marie and Madeleine Rebérioux, *The Third Republic From its Origins to the Great War: 1871–1914*. Trans J.R. Foster, Cambridge: Cambridge University Press, 1987.

Nelson, Bruce C. *Beyond the Martyrs: A Social History of Chicago's Anarchists*. New Brunswick: Rutgers University Press, 1984.

Rey, Claudine et al. *Petit dictionnaire des femmes de la Commune*. Paris: Le bruit des autres, 2013.

Ross, Kristin. *Communal Luxury: The Political Imaginary of the Paris Commune*. New York: Verso, 2015.

Rougerie, Jacques. *Paris Libre, 1871*. 2nd Ed. Paris: Seuil, 2004.

Traverso, Enzo. "Why the Commune Still Resonates, 150 Years Later." *Jacobin*, May 2021; https://jacobin.com/2021/05/paris-commune-150-anniversary-legacy.

Audio Recordings

Brécy, Robert, and Les Quatre Barbus. *La Commune de Paris 1871. Chants.* Paris: Serf, 1971

Clément, Jean-Baptiste (lyrics with diverse settings). *La Chansons de la Commune de Paris*. Ed. Adrienne Chaumont. Paris: Arion Music, 1981 (Naxos Online).

Les Ogres de Barback. *La Commune refleurira*. Alba La Romaine: Irfan, 2021. https://www.irfan.fr/artistes/discographie/159-la-commune-refleurira.htm

Tritsch, Jacques, and Group 17. *Chants de la Commune: Vivre libre ou mourir!* Paris: Le chant du monde, 1971.

Video Recording

Beloff, Zoë. Director and Designer. *Days of the Commune* by Bertolt Brecht. New York, March to May 2012. Video and other materials at: www. daysofthecommune.com.

Note: Weblinks active at the time of submission but cannot be guaranteed.

The Last Day of the Commune: Grand Panorama.
Poster by Charles Castellani.
Courtesy of the Bibliothèque Nationale, Paris.

PART 1: PROSE—LETTERS AND SPEECHES

This section introduces Pottier by way of two letters, which offer summary recollections of his life, work, and intellectual formation. The first is his letter of application in 1875 to the New York-based freemason lodge *Les Égalitaires*, which was published posthumously in the second edition of his *Chants révolutionnaires*. The second is a letter to Paul Lafargue, the husband of Marx's second daughter Laura, which Pottier wrote in 1884 once he had returned to Paris and re-established connections to former Communards. Although the letter initially accompanied Pottier's small collection—*Poésies d'économie sociale et chants socialistes révoluionnaires* [Social Economic Poems and Revolutionary Socialist Songs] published in 1884, the letter itself was not published until it appeared in a later edition of *Chants révolutionnaires* in 1937. Pottier's letter to the French freemasons in the U.S. briefly mentions the poverty that he endured in the initial years of exile but suggests that by 1875, he had found comrades able to help him. The letter of 1884, written nine years later in Paris, comes from a man who describes himself as old, poor, and exhausted, but grateful for the renewed interest in his work after the prize that he received from the *Lice Chansonnier* [Song Competition] in 1883.

The rest of this section comprises speeches that Pottier gave to sympathetic audiences along the U.S. East Coast from 1875 to 1879. The speech that commemorated the Commune on March 18, 1878, was printed by a branch of the Socialist Labor

Party in San Francisco, which indicates that Pottier's reputation had spread across the American continent, but this speech and the others included here were first collected by Pottier's younger contemporary Ernest Museux who included them in his book, *Eugène Pottier et son oeuvre*, first published in 1898, a decade after Pottier's death.

As secretary general of the French-speaking International in the U.S., Pottier also corresponded with London-based members of the International. Pierre Brochon includes these letters in his edition of Pottier's *Oeuvres completes* (1966) but, as they focus exclusively on raising funds to help the families of former Communards who had been sent to prison in the colony of French Caledonia in the Western Pacific Ocean, I have not included translations of them here. I have however added some information in brackets about dates and people mentioned by Pottier which is essential to the meaning of the texts.

Request for admission to the New York Lodge:
Les Égalitaires [The Egalitarians]

[This freemason lodge had been founded by French exiles from the Empire in the 1860s.]

Citizens,

I request admission to your lodge and the opportunity to participate in your work.

I know that you are a group of freethinkers who have scrapped tradition and who recognize no power above human Reason, which you deploy in pursuit of Truth and Justice.

I believe as you do that human happiness can have no other ground but reason. Scientific inquiry, free from the shackles of dogma, marches from day to day toward the discovery of the laws of our nature, and thus prepares the ground for the social code of conduct. To find its proper path, humanity must be created in our image. We must in other words become human singular and plural, though individual action and collective organization. The transformation of universal conflict into universal harmony can only come about through real equality, not the deceptive equality of liberal rights but equality of enlightenment and well-being.

With these few words, I offer a profession of faith and I trust that my life demonstrates my sincerity. I was born in Paris on October 4th, 1816. My mother was pious, my father a follower of Napoleon Bonaparte. I attended Catholic school until ten years old and then public school until twelve—I escaped this educational rut thanks only to my own reading later as a young man.

In 1832 [after the accession of the so-called bourgeois king Louis Phillipe], I became a republican. In 1840, I declared myself socialist. I played a small part in the revolutions of February and June 1848 and after the coup d'état [of Louis Bonaparte in 1851], I stuck to my guns as a socialist. Making peace with those who murdered Right and Justice would have meant selling out. After thirty years as a wage worker, I became a trained industrial [textile] designer in 1864. Industrial designers did not have a union; I prompted my colleagues to form one, and by the [Franco-Prussian] War, we had five hundred members and group affiliation with the International [Working People's Association].

In acknowledgement of my work with this movement, I was elected a member of the Paris Commune for the second *arrondisement* [district], where I held the office of district mayor. After the Versailles army captured the district on May 28th 1871, I moved to the 11th *arrondissment*. I accepted without reservation the revolutionary program of March 18th for the autonomy of the Commune and the emancipation of all workers. I trust that I did my duty.

During the struggle to defend the Commune when so many citizens lost their lives or their liberty, I was lucky to lose nothing more than my savings. I spent two years in exile in London and now I am in the United States, trying through work to alleviate my poverty and the effects of my banishment.

It was in Paris, during the last days of the struggle, when I encountered Freemasons who joined the Commune with great enthusiasm, planting their banners on our barricades that had been ripped apart by mortar shells. At that moment, I swore that one day I would join this phalanx of hard workers, and I now present myself at your lodge. Take me on!

Eugène Pottier—Freemason
238 East 30th Street [Paterson, NJ]
December 2, 1875

Letter to Paul Lafargue

*Note: I have abridged this letter to foreground Pottier's
account of his life and work, and references to contemporar-
ies that shaped his formation. I have added birth and death
dates for colleagues that Pottier mentions to highlight the age
range of Communards, and to distinguish between those who
managed to flee and those who died either on the barricades
or by execution in 1871.*

[. . .] I was born in Paris in 1816. I went to Catholic school
and at thirteen started my apprenticeship in my father's workshop at Saint-Anne:

*Asleep among the wood-shavings,
A left-handed clumsy dreamer.*

I learnt the rules of prosody from Restaud's old French
grammar which I found covered in mildew in a cabinet that was
about to be trashed. After that discovery, I copied and learned
by heart the songs of [Pierre-Jean de] Béranger [1780–1857; a
self-taught writer of popular lyrics], which served me well as a
substitute for Homer, Virgil, and Horace.

The "glorious days" of 1830 inspired me. It was then that I
wrote my first song, accompanied by the last barrage of bullets
shot by the Swiss during the taking of the Louvre [then still a
royal palace]. Naturally, the refrain was "Long Live Liberty!"
This rather commonplace effort was followed by a bunch of
others just as bad but a dozen or so were nonetheless printed
under the title "The Young Muse," the nickname given me at the
singing competition where I shared my efforts at age fourteen.
What happened to the five hundred copies? My comrades balled
them into spinning tops [...].

I then wrote half a dozen five-act verse dramas but, luckily
for me and everyone else, the rats devoured them all. Disgusted
by my father's trade, something that I regret today, I worked at
a neighborhood school as a grubby peon, earning half the wage
of the cleaning woman. Later, as an apprentice papermaker,

I wrote copy for the fine vaudeville and clever revues at the *Gymase d'enfants* in the Passage de l'Opéra. I was at this time a friend of Henri Murger (1822–81), and it was in our tenement that scenes from his *Vie de Bohème* were first played out. Unfortunately, my scripts went up in smoke in the fire that consumed the *Gymnase d'enfants*.

Around 1840, I wrote a song in the style of revolutionary poet Gracchus Baboeuf (1760–97). I gave the manuscript, now lost, to a communist comrade who had it printed, and it had a surprise success in Lyon and the Midi, where it apparently provoked "criminal agitators." […] but the events of 1848 really opened my heart and mind. I read Fourier and other socialists and wrote furiously.

[. . .] My songs were set to music but were apparently known only to intimate friends. [. . .]. Nonetheless I was apparently too revolutionary for "peaceful" democracy and my anarchist dynamite disturbed the powerful and respectable types.

In the meantime, I trained as an industrial designer. I was not the kind that followed the rules but rather freely used charcoal and a wayward paintbrush to sketch designs. I was an energetic creator but not much of a practical man. Nonetheless, I was by age thirty a supervisor in the best workshop in Paris, but under the guise of friendship the boss exploited me outrageously.

The failure of the 1848 revolution, especially the government's crimes against the June protests, ruined my health, and for twenty years I suffered from nerves and cerebral ischemia. Strictly speaking, I did not engage in political action, except in June 1848, when I was in the line of fire but avoided getting shot. At the time of Louis Bonaparte's coup d'état (1851) lung inflammation kept me from the protests.

Finally in 1870:

> *Poet, artist, laborer,*
> *I launched myself into the fray.*
> *And I thought that this endeavor*
> *Would bring us all a bright new day.*

At this point in time, I was doing well. I was the owner of the best design studio in Paris with an excellent clientele, which earned me a certain level of comfort. I provoked ire from my competitors because, as a member of the International, I encouraged their exploited employees to join the union which had five hundred members affiliated with the International.

During the Prussian siege of Paris in 1870, I joined the defense committee for the second *arrondissement* which paved the way for my election as a Commune delegate in March 1871. I was at the time already suffering from paralysis in the right hand, so I left the active delegate work to my younger colleague Jules Johannard (1843–92) and moved my office to the Stock Exchange, also in the second *arrondissement*. In April, during the debate around forming a Committee for Public Safety, I voted for it, despite my qualms, because I thought that the urgent situation demanded energy and unity in the fight against Versailles.

When the Versailles troops breached the Paris defenses and took the second *arrondissement*, I moved to the eleventh, where I joined Théophile Ferré (1845–71), Gustave Lefrançais (1826–1901), Édouard Vaillant (1848–1915), Eugène Varlin (1839–71), and Charles Delescluze (1809–71) during the last days of the battle for Paris.

[After the Commune fell], I was able to flee to England, where I stayed for two years. After that, I made it to the United States accompanied by my family. I stayed there for seven years and returned to France only with the amnesty of 1880, an old man and poor. I attempted to reestablish myself as a designer, but conditions in the industry had changed radically and I had no reserve capital. After two years of struggle, I was laid low by a stroke and paralysis along half my body and could no longer work.

The collection of poetry accompanying this letter is the work of a defeated man, despite the award from the *Lice Chansonnier*. In his preface to this volume, Gustave Nadaud, who sang my verses in 1848, tells a charming story about meeting me for the first time in 1848 and then encountering me again at the competition in 1883. In addition, I am attaching other works of mine that have been published.

Thank you kindly for your interest, my dear friend.

Your old Po-Po
Paris; May 29, 1884

Establishment of the Socialistic Labor Party Paterson, NJ; Section 1878

I have come to Paterson today to respond to your expressions of sympathy, after a previous visit with Lyon textile workers in exile, and another for the celebration of the Paris Commune anniversary on March 18, 1878. We are here for the same cause: Labor! I know only one cause: liberate labor, destroy slavery in its ultimate form, wage labor, and create humanity anew in a new world. This mission encompasses all the others. Since my arrival in Paterson, I seem to have escaped exile and found a little France to console and reinvigorate me. My friends, you have called, and I thank you for the invitation.

Greetings to Paterson, to Lyon, to St. Étienne and Saint-Chamond, greetings to the textile workers of Navette and the carders of Jacquard. Greetings above all to Croix-Rousse [garment-worker district of Lyon]. Listening to the clarion voices of all the trades, I hear also the revolutionary cry that forty years ago awakened my consciousness and made me a poet and a socialist.

All of you know this cry! The cry of people ground between the gears of capitalism. Whether it is written on our banners or in our hearts, it is the rallying cry of our youth—*live through work or die fighting*—in the early years of the reign of Louis-Phillippe [1830–48]. Bourgeois capitalism had arrived triumphant with the bourgeois king in 1830. Tossing aside the mask of liberalism under which it had challenged the restoration, it set in motion its system of extreme exploitation. When silk-workers immiserated by unemployment launched a petition to revive workers' cooperatives, Mr. Samuel, president of the National Assembly responded with complacent satisfaction: "The National Assembly is not responsible for giving work to laborers;" in other words, "work or die; we don't care." Pushed to breaking point by wage reductions—we know how that goes—the workers of Croix-Rousse put the following slogan on their black flag: "live through work or die fighting." They were denied work but faced the muzzle of a gun. Almost a hundred years ago, the French Revolution proclaimed the Rights of Man, but this proclamation was only a prologue. It is not enough to proclaim rights in the abstract; we must assure that all can exercise their rights. What use is the right to walk for paraplegics who have lost the use of their limbs?

Equal rights depend in practice on conditions of equality. This is the goal: let us find the shortest and most certain route to this goal. But this route, on which martyrs have preceded us, is littered with their dead bodies. Of the Revolutionary principles of 1789 and 1793, Liberty, Equality, Fraternity, the bourgeoisie has accepted only the first, Liberty, which it has interpreted to mean the omnipotence of capital and the crushing of the masses. The bourgeoisie has obliterated from its standard the word "equality," which it treats as a crime, and defames and persecutes those who support equal rights. As for fraternity, the bourgeois gestures towards it with charity, giving a hundred to those from whom it has stolen a thousand dollars. Capital's accelerated mode of production impoverishes the producer and exhausts humanity. The call of the poor in Croix-Rousse—live through work—is only a pipedream now. Under current wage conditions, working does not sustain life and we die of exhaustion. And the other point—die fighting—can we take that literally? Certainly, if the enslaved rally as they did in June 1848 or in May 1871, they can expect death in the battles that await them, defeat and massacre on a grand scale, the banning and deportation of the best of the rebels. In sum, to die fighting is not a normal life; we need to find something else less unendurable.

No-one becomes a revolutionary for the love of it. When people take to the streets, they do so propelled by a sense of purpose or compelled by despair. My friends, we need a better grasp of our project. What we have to change is not just people, but the entire organization of society; we need to correct the fundamental flaw in the relations of capital and labor. Today's society must be replaced by an organism that is smarter and more just and which will put capital and the means of production in the hands of workers. This battle is fought every day, every moment. It is not limited to the juvenile rage of the early days of revolution. This battle demands courageous and unending labor to organize all the oppressed classes for definitive enfranchisement once and for all.

This is what we are doing here in America; this is what people have done in earlier times. This is the universal task, the liberation and enfranchisement of labor, and we, you, all of us are the soldiers of this army. We, not the bosses, practice equality. Our forces grow more massive day by day, and the same blood, the blood of humanity, nourishes us all.

You all understand me. I am just the messenger reporting the battle, the battle to be joined by the Socialistic Labor Party. The platform may not in my view be complete, but I accept it. It rests on valid principles and may serve us as a prompt for the coming siege. These principles include the recognition that capital encompasses the globe, and everything that it contains—mines, pits, thoroughfares, and the massive apparatus of tramways, factories, steamers—has been made by workers the world over from generation to generation, and it should therefore remain social capital that belongs to all of us indivisible, not usurped by a few. Out of this transformation of the mode of production, a new society will emerge, capitalism will disappear, and capital return to the ranks of the workers themselves. And when capitalism goes, so too the army and the police, whose sole task has been to protect this usurped wealth, and the cult of the almighty dollar whose sole function has been to sanctify the appetites of the rich, to channel theft and fraud and to glorify the massacre of populations.

And so, my friends in Paterson and all my compatriots: when Germany, Russia, Norway are organized, when the fuse is ready to light up social revolution the world over, let us commit to the struggle. Let us show that the spirit of 1793 beats in our hearts, so that we will not leave unfinished the task of those before us. Through the inexhaustible quest for knowledge and enlightenment, humanity will cease to destroy itself by its own hand through civil and international war and, instead of dying in combat, the human family, transformed by wellbeing, science, and the arts, will live through work.

Speech delivered on the anniversary of the Commune, March 18, 1878

To the families of the proletariat, to citizens of toil and misery, citizens of the realm of anxiety that makes us old before our time, citizens of hardship that exhausts us; to the cheerful and carefree brood of socialism: greetings. I come to you with a double remit: for the dead in the Paris Commune, and for the living in the Socialistic Labor Party.

Let us speak first in the name of the dead, but is the Commune really dead? In the presence of those mowed down by machine guns, the heroes shot at Satory Prison, the exiled raging at Nouméa in French Caledonia, who can doubt it?

The Commune is dead; the Communards buried in the coats of the volunteer National Guard, buried in such haste that they lay dying, barely covered with the earth that fell into their ditches. In that gloomy night, in the glow of the stars, their hands so frightfully raised, to what Justice did they appeal?

To divine Justice?

But astronomy, exploring myriads of worlds that people infinite space, long ago evicted God the father and his sainted family.

To human justice?

But the conquered did not find robed and bewigged judges presiding in the courts, only lackeys and executioners.

Did they appeal to avengers?

But the mob danced on around the dead, with Holy Churchmen in lacy collars, cassocks gallantly flowing, pitilessly intoning *Te Deum* to accompany the massacre.

This was the ghoul of capitalism, seized by a sort of remorse, while calculating to see if the extermination of workers would lead to higher wages for the rest.

And the gang of clerics, while trampling on Republican armbands in red-white-and-blue, loudly shouted Victory, with bellicose cowardice.

Did the dead appeal to History?

But that history was being written by the Papist Louis

Veuillot and by Hippolyte de Villemessant of *Le Figaro*. And U.S. Ambassador Eli Washburn regurgitated this puke in his speeches.

And the future?

The future was not to be! The past was hot on its heels and brought with it enslavement of body and mind, medieval stupefaction and the plague of Caesarism. And the Communard's dead hand raised in lonely defiance against triumphant Versailles appeared to protest in the name of humanity enslaved by centuries of oppression and degradation.

So, citizens, here we are on the seventh anniversary of the Commune. The dead are not dead; their red blood pulses in our hearts. History will speak and judge the judges; as for the future, the avengers arise, and we are not the ones who are afraid. You know the proverb—*fight first, explain after*.

After the battle, the question. *What, Commune, do you want? Why were you massacred and defamed?* As Claude-François Denecourt paraphrased Giambattista Basile, "defame, defame; slander always sticks" (1875). Calumny comes from the enemies of socialism but what remains is often the defamer's confusion of the defamer. An hour comes when an irreproachable person who been defamed puts a foot in the manure and marches head high basking in the sun of political esteem.

Let us leave aside calumny, the slime of slugs. Let us explain our position. Some say that the Commune was a coward's protest and a treasonous response to the siege of Paris; others say that you, the Communards, wanted to secure self-government for Paris, as for the United States, by citizen election of municipal government. Still others say that the monarchical-clerical coalition that was exposed on May 16, 1870, [by Louis-Bonaparte's meddling with the Prussian Hohenzollern succession, alleged to have provoked the Franco-Prussian war] wanted to undo the achievements of the bourgeois revolution of 1789 and overturn the Republic, our protector, and that Paris thwarted this attempt by proclaiming the Commune. And finally, there are those who think that the Commune was the prelude to a social revolution equivalent to the astronomical revolution of Copernicus and Galileo, a movement that exchanged the arbitrary rulings of authoritarianism for the scientific laws of solidarity.

Which of these explanations is true?

All of them! The Revolution of March 18th, 1871 was all of these things; that is its glory. It put into practice the principles of the International, which produced the Socialistic Labor Party. It was the railway switch that changed our direction. We can get to our destination only by passing through the stations—from mutual aid, equal exchange, planned services, at the first stage; to collectivism, that is the nationalization of productive and circulating capital—soil, mines, factories, machinery, canals, railways, steamers, communication systems. And certainly, we should not stop there. Our ideal is limitless expansion but the most impatient among us were content with this much progress. Only after the first strikes of the piston can the train begin to move full steam ahead. Meanwhile, those reactionaries who provoked the catastrophe of derailment describe themselves as conservatives.

Two questions remain for the Commune and for Communards: who are your avengers? What is their task? My avengers are above all the proletarians stripped of the products of their labor, those who produce without consuming for the benefit of those who consume without producing. In other words, the vast masses, except for a notorious minority that should disappear or return to the ranks.

The caterpillar should become a bee.

For we will treat you as traitors, capitalist usurers, thieves! You, pamphleteers, charlatans, priests. Liars! You, kings and Caesars, bearers of sabers and togas, assassins! You disgrace the social contract. The head that thinks and the body that acts do not forge contracts with vermin who are outside the law.

My avengers are those great minds who struggle passionately for social justice, who are not satisfied with a society of heartless types who every morning shamelessly observe bankruptcies and stock-market swings, suicides prompted by wretchedness.

This society tolerates the starvation of families shivering in their damp infested straw beds while the Vatican pontificates about the poor giving their souls to the Lord and gives two hundred million to pay off debt to the Rothschilds.

This is a society that rests on the backs of small shop-owners possessed by the idea of individual property like the shell envelops the oyster, a society of crooks that take refuge in the bosom of the Church, as they stand guard in front of their locked safes with a crucifix held like a bayonet.

My avengers are all those who like you are members of *Trades Unions* [English in original], of resistance cells, and cooperatives. I speak of you, the Socialistic Labor Party, of your activism, your solidarity, your respect for the honor of all your members, the workers reflecting on social problems, the children whose eyes light up with reason after having been hollowed out by dogma. You are the pen that flows over the paper, the paper on the rolling press, the train on the rails, the telegram on the wire, the infinite network and the perpetual fusion of all rays, all minds, all nationalities.

On American soil, this network puts the hand of the French worker in the hand of the German, their glasses filled with foaming beer or sparkling wine, toasting universal harmony!

And what is the task of all these avengers? Creating the future?

Up until now, we have paid dearly for a ready-made future, a future tailored for all the peddlers who sell the legislative handcuffs and muzzles that have trapped us, necks exposed and sleeves as well, tied us up in this straitjacket.

In times to come, we will make our own future to our own measure, out of whole cloth.

Do we not have a double plan for social organization? The human being, in strength an organism singular and multiplied, moving together to the same goal; what is life but a living commune?

The universe, of which we are but a sample, does it not

manifest the same shape, same laws, same principles?

Air, water, heat, light, electricity: individual or collective property?

Let us return to Nature after centuries of separation: she will spread her green carpet, light her lamps, and all the wonders of science and art; let us kill the fatted calf for this festival of the free and equal.

Citizens, this evening's celebration is prelude to our splendid future, and it is this future to which the Commune's National Guards, shot and buried alive, raised their prophetic hands. If the telephone, this recent miracle of human invention, links us this minute with all the cities of the United States and the capitals of Europe where the disinherited celebrate March 18th, if these exploding ovations resonate in this hall, may we see these walls crumble, and after them the walls of the old society as we magnify our thunderous cry of deliverance: *Vive la Commune!*

Speech to the Socialistic Labor Party, Paterson: December 27, 1878

Citizens!

Do you know what a splendid idea you have here, of closing the year with a family holiday? Tied down for twelve months, we have dragged the ball and chain of toil and monotonous chores, the burden of unemployment, privations of all kinds, material and intellectual, anxieties about the future; in short, the weight of the galley-slave emerging from the depths of misery.

Balls and chains, anxieties and woes, we have checked those at the door and will pick them up again tomorrow but here we are together, the Paterson comrades and their happy companions. We have before us a full night of festivities to enjoy; we will draw wine from the same barrel, which will revive and fortify us. This socialist festival in this hall decorated with the red flag; this gala where our hearts begin to beat, is a prelude to the magnificent life that the future reserves for our children. Raise your glasses, let them ring in fraternity; here we are no longer French, American, or German; whether old or young; men or women; all of us are socialists.

Let us toast Rabelais's wine, Gambrinus's foamy bock! Let us for once enjoy life radiant and abundant!

Let the electricity generated by your sympathetic energy enhance our family affections, fire up our spouses and our lovers, so that next year at the same time we will double our numbers with a new generation of socialist babies. We will teach them in their cradles the rallying cry of the disinherited so that our choir will reunite our two hemispheres: *Vive la Commune!*

But, my friends, without wishing to sound like a prophet of doom or a bird of ill fortune, I do have to say that I see red on the horizon. In Germany, people are being persecuted, expelled, exiled; newspapers suppressed; books burned as in the Middle Ages. The Tsar of all the Russians has depopulated Moscow and St. Petersburg to fill up Siberia. Switzerland no longer offers refuge. The Iron Chancellor [Otto von Bismarck of the German Second Reich], the emperors who rule by the fist, the petty tyrant windbags, the whole holy retinue of throne and altar supported by the idle aristocrats, the greedy capitalists, the police with batons, and those disguised as journalists, everything and everyone that is corrupt, bought, prostituted, cowardly, or fierce, is rising up and in league to bring us a war of extermination.

France is asleep, exhausted by a phantom pregnancy, drugged by opportunists. Around her, word spreads that she is bleeding out and that heroic remedies are necessary to save socialist Europe. Over here, in the United States, do you think that you can go it alone?

The three large capitalist parties appear prepared to fight it out, as is their wont, but tomorrow they will see their funds at risk and will form a holy trinity, three united as a single vampire. Do you not see that they are already reaching for Ulysses S. Grant's mighty sword, and that the bogeyman will be back from Versailles to stuff his big bag with disobedient brats, with communists who spoil the digestion of the good folks in Washington and Wall Street?

The prompts for this persecution are the attempts at repression by the emperors and kings who have come to power in Berlin, Naples, and Madrid. Even though this is a thorny subject, let us speak of these attempts and, above all, of their source. Who is arming these men who appear not to know one another and yet are acting in concert? Remember the juridical maxim: "he who stands to profit, commits the crime." Not that I would call it a crime to topple monarchs. Whoever claims to be above the law is an outlaw, and when brave men who penetrate the jungle at risk for their lives to chase the tiger, I would not take the side of that ferocious beast.

Returning to that maxim—who stands to profit from these efforts? Only those who want to redirect the fury of ignorant people against the Internationalists. The priest and the statesman; the priest, above all the Jesuit, have already proven their mettle, and the knives of Jacques Clément [fanatic Catholic partisan during the religious wars in sixteenth-century France] and of [François] Ravaillac [Catholic assassin of the ecumenical king Henri IV in 1610] come from his factory.

As for the statesman, his name is Bismarck; with one terrible, odious phrase, he has pummeled reason and justice, and spat on humanity. You know that phrase—*might makes right.* That phrase justifies the villainy of the conqueror who, at the head of the army, robs a people as a highwayman robs a carriage. It is also in the interest of the manipulator Bismarck to strike fear in the hearts of the crowned heads of Europe to enlist them in his crusade.

But despite Bismarck's villainy, *The New York Herald* blames the Blanquists [followers of anarchist Louis-Auguste Blanqui] exiled in London. The purpose of this infamy can only be to prolong and worsen the conditions of captivity suffered by Citizen Blanqui. I do not need to prove the falsity of this rumor which appears to come from *Le Figaro*. [...] Once again, the old accusation: socialists are allegedly the enemies of the family, of order, and of property, who want to turn society upside down. Indeed, we do—with enthusiasm.

Starting with the family: before we tell you how we understand the family, how do the powerful understand it? What is this institution? Home for foundling children. And these well-stocked night bazaars of lust on the doorsteps of every stock exchange? And these doctors who offer wealthy clients the means to prevent maternity? And their morality? Adultery?

Don't speak of family but instead of the man whose compensation provides for all material needs, the woman, household provider without exception; the public, professional, religion-free—and, essential—attractive school for the child in the care of the commune and the parents; for the old, rest and wellbeing: do you offer these benefits? No? well, then, you have no family!

As to the accusation that we want to destroy religion: no, that task is not ours. That is the work of science; astronomy has toppled God to reveal instead an infinity of suns in infinite space. Physics, chemistry, geology have turned the pages of the bible into paper tigers.

Science mocks clerics of all sects, with their miracles, their pilgrimages, their festivals immaculate or otherwise, all this clownish prattle that makes Jesus Christ a buffoon, whispering their humbug. Drop the curtain; the farce is done. Philosophy and poetry, not religion, will reveal the unknown to humanity. And what of order? Order! Do you mean the order found in the cemeteries containing the crowds mowed down by machine guns? We understand instead that the real order in hearts and minds is created by satisfying physical, intellectual, and spiritual needs; by the harmony of interests between the individual and the unlimited range of the general good.

And finally, property? As [Pierre-Joseph] Proudhon said: *Property is theft.* We go further, observing the fraudulent confiscation of surplus labor and its consequences in the death and misery of the population: *Property is murder.*

You the rich are complicit in the murder of our children, and we ask that social science redress the balance and proceed to liquidate your assets. Turn society upside down? Not quite, but disorder undoes artificial cohesion, just as a chemical reaction creates a precipitant. And for this cannibal society in which the fat can eat the little people, we would substitute *the social whole.*

As for making war on capital, that's a big lie. For, what is capital? It is the globe itself, with all the riches in its depths, and those that flow to the surface. The forces of nature at the disposal of science, human muscle, wind, falling water, expanding gases, steam, electricity; everything that remains of human endeavor; the universal toolkit created by the worker; the ideas that bubble up inside the brains of inventors; the talent for production in the hand of the artist and the artisan.

It is the entire sacred arsenal of science and the arts, museums, and libraries. It is, to coin a phrase, the past that has engendered the present, and the present that will engender the future. All that is capital and socialists are not at war with it; on the contrary, they treat it as their redemption.

What about war on capitalists? Vanderbilt, or Rothschild? What difference does it make who these men are, or others like them? It is the system that we wish to destroy because capitalism is more than a few monopolist millionaires. The shoemaker is a capitalist exploiter of his leather, the tailor of his cloth. Whoever monopolizes the smallest atom of primary matter is a capitalist if he demands that we pay him a ransom, profit, to delivery what he calls his merchandise. Human beings have a right to compensation for their work but no more than the equivalent of the surplus value which they have added to the primary material. No one at no time has the right to possess the substance of nature itself. Nature is not for sale or for purchase. The day when workers understand this universal law, the social question will be resolved; labor will be exchanged for equivalent labor. [...]

So, socialists: who is your enemy? No single individual. We seek rather to replace the system of disorderly competition which operates in the shadows fomenting unemployment, bankruptcy, ruin, with cooperative ownership, mutual aid, and a bank of exchange. We want to demonetize gold, silver, and useless banknotes with credits per labor hour, backed by the guarantee of nationalized corporations that would collectively hold the assets of society. Under these conditions, the so-called *eternal society* of monopolists, capitalists, parasites, uncountable middlemen, kings, bureaucrats, clergy stripped of their tithes, armies without credit, all would evaporate and go up in smoke.

You all would eviscerate your enemies then?

No! They would simply join the ranks of workers, as the nobility joined those of the bourgeoisie on pain of starvation after the Revolution, since their assets would no longer be worth enough to buy a basic loaf of bread.

So, my good friends, instead of fighting socialism, follow our motto: we want capital

but not capitalists! We all have potential capital but we want to rid ourselves of the capitalist system that exploits us.

And you socialists, pioneers of the future, strong people who seek grand tasks or those who desire peace and happiness, old people who want repose, young people who strive to join the world of science, all of us are part of the same mind and the same being, Humanity, sharing a vision of the ideal world and marching towards light and happiness on the road to justice, guided by the same motto: Capital we want, but not capitalists!

Eugène Pottier. Caricature by Hippolyte Mailly. Published
in *La Commune* 1871. Courtesy, Museum of the Hôtel de Ville, Paris

PART 2: SELECTED POEMS
AND SONGS

This section features selected poems, songs, and ballads written by Pottier at successive stages of his active life, from the 1848 revolutions, at which time he was already a seasoned activist at thirty-two, through his participation in the governance of Paris Commune of 1871, exile in the U.S., and his last years in Paris from 1880 to his death at the age of seventy-one in 1887. While many of these texts merit the label that he gave them—*Chants révolutionnaires* or revolutionary songs—several poems mix revolutionary fervor with elegiac reflection on the (perhaps temporary) failure of revolution. Still others, especially those from the so-called second empire (1852–1870) declared by Napoleon's nephew Louis Bonaparte a.k.a. Napoleon III, express critical views of the wonders of the age, from the Universal Expositions to scientific inventions, to the state of the global environment, ecological as well as political.

I have divided the selections into six parts:

1. *1848: February and June Uprisings*; these poems respond especially to the democratic and egalitarian aspirations of the June rebels.

2. *Counter-revolution, 1849–50*: these works reflect the uncertain period after the failure of revolution as Bonaparte was consolidating power as president of the National Assembly but before he declared himself Emperor in 1852.

3. *The Second Empire, 1852–70* brings together elegies on failed or dormant revolution with poems celebrating technological breakthroughs, such as the Universal Exposition of industrial design and the trans-Atlantic cable (1867) that enabled news about the Commune to travel at telegraphic speed.

4. *The 1871 Commune and After:* the poems and songs in this section, which begins with *L'Internationale*, were written after the fall of the Commune, from Pottier's last days in Paris through his brief sojourn in Britain, but they vividly recall the aspirations of those seventy-two days, while acknowledging the suffering after the Commune's collapse.

5. *American Exile* includes poems written while Pottier was in the United States. Some are elegies for the Commune, but others suggest a more optimistic focus on progress, from a portrait of his daughter as a child of the Commune to poems that deploy images from astronomy and other sciences to capture the universality of political aspirations to equality.

6. *The Third Republic* includes poems that depict the ongoing struggle of the working-classes in the Third French Republic and satirical treatments of the ruling classes and their apologists, such as the political economists of the *Collège de France*, the most elite of France's tertiary education institutions, known then and now as the *grandes écoles*.

Although his poems respond to particular moments and events from 1848 on, Pottier's lifelong preoccupation with the long arc of revolution saturates his entire oeuvre. While he sharply attacked the elites of the Third Republic for alleged indifference to social inequality and to the outright poverty suffered by the majority of citizens despite the republican presumption that France led the world in liberty, equality, and fraternity, his poems also acknowledge those elements of Communal thought that left their imprint on French society. His poems highlight above all the resolutely anti-clerical cast of the republic, which expanded public, secular education for all children; the rights of working people, women as well as men, to a living wage and social wellbeing; and the amnesty granted Communards, which enabled him and his comrades to return home and to publish their criticism of the slow progress towards equality and solidarity.

1. 1848: February and June Uprisings

Estates General of Labor
Dedicated to the Luxemburg Delegation (March 1848)
To the tune of *La Marseillaise*

Bosses, workers, brains, and artists,
The human hive starts up in congress.
Surrounded still by egoists,
We will clear a path for progress.
France, at last, is unrestrained,
Heart, mind, and each two hands
Labor for our human gains
As a seamstress sews her bands.
      To work, Citizens! Now or never!
      Labor rules, let's march forever (2)

Order, honor, vigilance,
Our workers are the very best,
People of intelligence
You will be our workshop heads.
Separate, we rob our brother,
Once rivals, we now join together.
From our sun new rays for all,
The clock will strike a wake-up call.
      To work, Citizens! Now or never!
      Labor rules, let's march forever (2).

What! Sweating for the lowest wage?
Is that not the bread of scorn?
Those that cultivate the sage,
Not allowed to glean the corn!
After fifty years of plucky courage
Doing tasks both foul and tough,
We leave to heirs, our kin and such,
Mere misery as heritage

To work! Citizens! Now or never!
Labor rules, let's march forever (2).

You usurers have no faith, no guts,
Bolted like your safes of steel,
Crows all nipping at our butts,
Gnaw our dead as their next meal.
Do not wait—drive out the blight,
Famine and our deep despair.
Look—it's up to us now to aspire
With numbers to claim our due by right.
   To work! Citizens! Now or never
   Labor rules, let's march forever (2).

Holy love of mother country,
Inspiring us until the end,
May cure us all humanity
Of want and ignorance, my friend.
May our time be well endowed,
When God permits, we stop and rest.
At end of day, we say "my best."
May this avowal be allowed.
   To work! Citizens! Now or never!
   Now Labor rules, let's march forever (2).

First published in an anthology called *Chansons de l'atelier [Songs from the Workshop]*
Signed "Eugène Pottier, worker"

Liberty, equality, fraternity—and fun (1848)

To the tune: *Amusez-vous, belles.* Published in *Songs from the Workshop* (1848).

The Re-pub-lic
Is pa-ci-fic:
Do not shun us
But support us
  Amuse yourselves!
  Disguise yourselves!
  Rich people—
  Disguise yourselves!
  Don't be mean!
  Have some fun!
More bread is what we need,
And your charity should feed us.
But the trade in gold is doing better.
  (Amuse yourselves etc.)
A donation we beg you please,
A polka for humanity
A cancan for your charity.
  (Amuse yourselves etc.)

Women, parties
And toilettes,
Flower, silk, dressy pumps
Substitute for bread in lumps.
  (Amuse yourselves, etc.)

If at the fancy dance,
The mask displays a happy face,
It also covers all regrets.
  (Amuse yourselves etc.)

Drop the dreams,
Gossips, schemes.
We will dispense with terror--
By terrorizing terror!
  (Amuse yourselves etc.)

Misers blame the miserable
The poor who flee the hound,
As hunger moves, the wolf comes round.
   (Amuse yourselves etc.)

Proletarian my kin,
We will vote, await the finish.
Dare I say: don't be famished.
   (Amuse yourselves etc.)

Laborers on stone and paving,
No dreaming now! It's time to strike!
What are they now craving?
So early must they arise.
   (Amuse yourselves etc.)

Poverty is not a crime,
And if we could allow the rhyme,
Say the rich's riches
Won't make them bitches.
   (Amuse yourselves etc.)

Killing time to kill ennui (June 1848)
   For Emile Zola

The factory's foul and full of gloom,
The air is rank, the window black;
Still, I work in this same room,
Like a squirrel scurrying back.
My arteries are full of lead,
I rust and rust in all the grime,
Drinking plonk soaked up my bread.
   It's time, it's time to kill off time.

Oh, to live in Africa,
Like a lion roaming free.
In politics, not so wise
But I need it just to be.
The road explodes with fire and guns;
People: march to crush ennui.
  It's time, it's time, to kill off time!

June 1848

  To Courbet, member of the Commune

We must die, so let us go! The error lies between us.
Bow our heads and cross our arms,
In wages and in life, they fleece us.
We've lost our right to live, they mean us harm.
Let us die with all good grace,
We unsettle those who stuff their face.
At their banquet denied a place.
  We must die!
  Comrades, we must die!

We must die! No work around
The workshop, the steam machine,
The fields, the sun, and the ocean sound
Have closed down? Capital has lost its sheen.
Our guts are hollow when stocks crash or rise,
Frozen veins where blood should flow,
Not even spades to dig our holes.
  We must die!
  Comrades we must die!

We must die but there's plenty wheat,
We must die with grapes on vine,
We must die but ants will eat,

And insects in grain are doing fine.
The sky arcs over all creation,
Why then must we endure cessation?
Nature's sealed, to our frustration.
   We must die!
   Comrades, we must die!

Desperation will drain the breast:
No more milk! Citizen baby, die!
Your father's wrong, your mom depressed,
The infant poor no right to thrive.
But the fever's up and we will rise.
Let cannon come, and their spies.
Guns be quicker than starvation, lies.
   We must die!
   Comrades, we must die!

2: Counter-Revolution: 1849–50

Newton's Apple (1849)

Newton to himself did ponder,
Reflecting on new shoots in May,
How to solve a crucial number:
The universe's eternal a?
Drifting thoughts on life and death,
His gaze a-wandering through the air,
When suddenly an apple fell
And lit a spark inside his head.
Falling apple said to him:
"I submit to gravity.

"How often wandering in the wood
Must we take note of Nature's good?
How many acorns, chestnuts fall,
Before we grasp their guiding law?
Nature's wealth behind a veil,
Hidden, not comprehended.
Science reveals through much travail
What daily God has us extended.

"My weight obeys a rule transparent,
Because the logic is the same
That links the moon up to the planet,
Planet, sun, and global frame.
Each sphere must orbit in its place,
As your blood must circulate,
Prompted by the heart's embrace,
Will jolt the mind to cogitate."

I understand it now, so Newton said,
Holding suns inside his head
Through gravity the apple's part

Plays as does the human heart.
But, alas, he could not see
The force that crimps mobility,
The laws that oppress society
And do not allow us to be free.

Will he plumb the depths of life?
No, he was not bold enough,
Like a fly on pane of glass
He sees the sky but cannot pass.
The apple falling every day
Cannot show us the whole way,
But this world embattled still must move
Towards our freedom and our love.

My Property (1849)

I lay no claim to any walls
But space and everything that moves,
The burning plain and the dark woods.
Pity millionaires behind their walls.

I have a stick, a shirt, a hat of straw,
Great big clogs, a dog, a book,
Every day at morning song,
I set out to survey my goods.

As I play the good proprietor
To wild oats, blue flax and yellow corn,
They bend again towards the earth,
Swayed by the wind their seeds are borne.

The opera has no sound more fresh,
Nor décor prettier than my trees,

My mossy stall, my crisp green leaves,
All praise to tenors in the breeze.

Your treasures blowing in the wind,
Diamonds, silverware arrayed.
Come and see the rose-hued dew
Glitter in the sunny ray.

Like a knife plunged in your domain,
Bourgeois, my eyes will rob you blind,
My pal the breeze will blow my way
The perfume of your fragrant lime.

The land the law may give to you,
Yet to accommodate my verse,
I lay my claims from star to star
To stride across the universe.

> *I lay no claim to any walls*
> *But space and everything that passes*
> *Mine: burning plain and the dark woods.*
> *Pity millionaires behind their walls.*

The Death of a World (1849)
To Benoît Malon, member of the Commune

In azure seas of swimming stars
Our human eyes plumb the dark
Infinity may yet reveal
to our spirit, inner eye,
Celestial bodies, stars with souls,
Their whirling orbs with joy or sorrow
Love unites these kindred fires.
   Weep, you suns; a world expires.

In an age with no hunger seen,
The globe could turn in liberty,
Folks united, happy, free,
Could reap its riches infinitely.
But our mistakes have caused disaster,
Rotted the planet ever faster,
Stars and world in a state so dire
  Weep, you suns; a world expires.

Rivers of blood as war's unleashed,
Stopped and gagged, ideas enmeshed,
Moneybags gnaws our distress,
Like a cannibal chews human flesh.
With awful hands he holds the knife,
He butchers all in sacrifice
To vengeful God, souls afire.
  Weep, you suns, a world expires.

But still our blood in veins does pound,
The spark revives our flesh and mind,
The grand accord of human will
Passions divine in us instill.
But the burden lies, the soul deceived,
The ax that amputates cannot heal;
Prometheus genius—amputee
  Weep, you suns, a world will die.

Regretful sobs drift on the air
From the giant a final sigh,
The world, a corpse, is done, destroyed,
Tossed forever in the void.
The universe in darkest night
May search for bones beyond our sight.
Graveyard of globes, the Milky Way
  Weep, you suns, our world will die.

3: The Second Empire 1852–1870

Who will avenge her? (December 1851)

The Republic is dead.
Past her coffin we are led.
Her gravedigger am I then—?
But who will avenge her?
Her gravediggers, that we were,
My heart as well I do inter,
Those who survive, we will see her,
I will wait 'til she returns.
Those who survive, we will see her,
We will see the earth that bears her,
We will hear the hammer praise her.
    Work will nourish us
    And flourish the rose.

In the leafy autumn,
In the moistened earth,
I alone will dig her berth.
But who will avenge her?
I alone will clear the sand,
As I sing, am I mad?
Those who survive, we will see her,
We will see her resurrected.
Those who survive, we will see her,
We will see the earth that bears her,
We will hear the hammer praise her.
    Work will nourish us
    And flourish the rose.

The New Era (1860)
  To Vladimir Gagneux, representative

Labor, your stolen fields
Have been usurped by misery.
From the earth we'll have our yields
When we work collectively.
  Our day will come, and we'll take flight.
  Let labor, justice and love's light.
  Bring us to a future bright.

Your railways bring expanding trade.
Put your resources in our trains
That traverse the fertile land,
As does our blood run through our veins.
  Our day will come and we'll take flight.
  Let labor, justice, and love's light.
  Bring us to a future bright.

From volcanos underground
Our new machines must draw their force,
Impart a power now unbound,
Free all slaves to choose their course.
  Our day will come and we'll take flight.
  Let labor, justice, and love's light.
  Bring us to a future bright.

Steamers cross from sea to sea,
From equator to the poles.
Abundance and productivity
Shared by all, the world a whole.
Our day will come and we'll take flight.
Let labor, justice, and love's light.
Bring us to a future bright.
Now cables laid across the deep
Link human voices with their lines.

We'll sound as clear as mouth to ear
Surpassing fire and flare as vital signs.
Our day will come and we'll take flight.
Let labor, justice, and love's light.
Bring us to a future bright.

The Exposition (Exhibition of industrial arts, 1861)

Human genius, breath alive,
Your creation on display,
The crystal palace like a hive,
Full of treasures of the day.

It rises up above the ground,
Truly wondrous to behold,
Illuminates the trinity
Of Art and Science and Industry.
Visitors come in waves and waves,
Come, all you ears, and you eyes.
Invention now will show the way,
Marvels, wonders will arise.

Heaven, ardent observation,
Contemplates our vast creation.
The man of genius is sure to serve us
As a guide with animation.
Nature is our source for labor,
Invites us to refine her plan,
This a day for us to savor,
Enhancing our full lifespan.

High above, the stained-glass pane,
The transept's length compels our eye
To admire this poem of hues,
Garden of lines and of delight,

The sparkle of the dew at dawn.
Amazing, a wonderland!
When a breeze passes by the sun,
The colors shine like gems: how grand!

Glowing skies and sparking water
Animate our bolts of silk,
Inspire us to match bird and feather,
Jacquard smooth and soft as milk.
Artisans, extend a hand!
Your glory will transform our fate.
We will make the banquet grand,
By sporting a new purple coat.

People harness giant forces,
From myth to fact the fire will reach.
Underneath the ocean courses
A cable carrying human speech.
In the depths the most obscure,
The modern lens shines its light.
Ingenuity will ensure
That our projects come out right.

Artists, all things there for you—
Forests, sea, and rosy flesh,
History's sorrows, madness too—
To capture ideals in the mesh.
Your task it is to infuse life
In blocks of marble, canvas frame,
To shine a light on our dark sky
Like a group of stars aflame.

And you, our dead whose names appear,
Engraved in stone, to honor pacts,
You ancestors, your thoughts endure,
Eternally, as science facts.

Trees whose pollen snows the ground,
Germinate the stronger seed,
But can we be shoots that should abound,
If our roots are good and dead?

What the Bread Says (1867)
  To Léon Ottin

I hear the jokers ponder: what—
Does bread say when it's cut?
This may well be easy to recap,
Not so eloquent as soup.
Wheat or buckwheat, that's the grain
For our stomachs to sustain
  Do you know what bread says?
  Do you know what bread says?
  Bread says: Eat, for I am life!

Who knows the price of dough—
Apart from cattle as they low
And the man with sunburn peeled,
Who plows a furrow in the field?
All the rich, so vain and idle
Savor bread without due title.
  Do you know what bread says?
  Do you know what bread says?
  Bread says: glory be for those who work!

Our commitment leads to change,
Bitter tasks demand exchange.
Giving birth so many times
Mothers bleed with each confine,
To revivify a weakened soul
And push towards our human goal.
  Do you know what bread says?
  Do you know what bread says?

I have been right through the mill!

Worker, when will you see it straight?
Your baker is a usurer.
No more than the day or air
Bread will not be sold in miser's measure,
When we end all misery.
  Do you know what bread says?
  Do you know what bread says?
  Bread says: make your own big batch!

Absorbing all of nature's bounty,
Pumping blood from vital sap,
Our bodies, selves, reborn, renewed.
Nourished, strengthened, lap by lap,
As these sources by osmosis
Feed healthy flesh and thinking brain.
  Then will bread speak to assure us:
  This is the product of my grain!

Women on Strike! (1867)

Another Maid will rise among us,
Protesting women who will say:
"Until we achieve universal peace,
Love and more we hold at bay."

  Down with war, we won't be laid.
  Women have to break the blade.
  Mock the lover and the spouse,
  Until disarmament is ours.

Devoted sweethearts, brunette and blonde,
As citizens of all estates
Must put an end to spilling blood.
We will stage a coup d'état!

Because all war wants more and more
Heaps of mutilated and the dead,
We women who bring life abjure
Our vows and lock ourselves instead.

This noble role as chaste coquette
We will assert with this threat:
Scratch the claim of sex conquest
And the right to kiss and pet!

Sir, your concubine I am not.
You can manage in the loo.
The marriage bed has gone to pot,
The reason is a tax that's due.

Mothers, spouses, that we are.
Let them grumble. Men who destroy,
Who shoot to kill, and more,
Do not deserve to sire a boy.

If you must let loose your troops
Let them pursue tigresses, apes.
We are no longer in your coop,
To bear cannon fodder after rape.

God of peace, please bless this strike,
And to honor new times and neighbors
We will create new life your like,
When we return to our labors.

> *Down with war, we won't be laid.*
> *Women have to break the blade.*
> *Mock the lover and the spouse,*
> *Until disarmament is ours.*

4: The 1871 Commune and After

The Internationale (late May 1871)
  To citizen Gustave Le Français, member of the Commune

  The English version below owes debts to the IWW Songbook
  (1909), The Weekly People (1924), and Billy Bragg (1990).
  The original published in Chants révolutionnaires (1887)
  begins with the refrain, hence the order here. See Part Three
  for the French text, along with the cited English translations.

  Now comrades come rally,
  Let all take their place!
  The International working-class
  Unites the human race. (IWW Songbook—revised).

Stand up, you hostages to hunger,
Stand up, all outcasts on the earth.
Reason thunders in its crater,
And a better world's in birth.
Let's blot out all superstition,
Subdued masses, heed the call.
Our world is changing at foundation.
We were naught, we shall be all.

  Come brothers and sisters,
  Our struggle carries on.
  The Internationale
  Unites the world in song (Billy Bragg)

There are no saviors here to help us
No god, no master, no appeal.
Workers, we alone shall save us,
We create the commonweal.
Strip the thieves of stolen booty,
Release from prison every soul.

We ourselves must prime the gears,
Strike the iron and wrest control.

Refrain:
Now comrades come rally,
Let all take their place!
The International working-class
Unites the human race.
Come brothers and sisters,
Our struggle carries on.
The Internationale
Unites the world in song.

The state's oppressive and the law's a ruse.
Taxation weighs us down.
The rich today still pay no dues,
And our rights as good as none.
Long enough have we been babied,
Equality's new law will write:
"No rights without your duties
And no duties without rights."

Refrain: Now comrades …

Ugly in their brutal power
Stand lords of mine and press and rail
They perform no useful labor
But steal the yield of workers' toil.
In the coffers of these bosses
All the world's abundance thrown,
In demanding restitution
The people only claim their own.

Refrain: Now comrades…

Toilers in field and shop together,
Solidarity to all who work.
The earth belongs to those who labor.
Get lost, you idler and you shirk!
How many on our flesh have feasted?
But if the vultures and the vampires go,
Vanish from the morning sky,
The sun would still arise and glow.

> *Refrain:*
> *Now comrades come rally*
> *Let all take their place*
> *The International working-class*
> *Unites the human race*
> *Come brothers and sisters*
> *As struggle carries on*
> *The Internationale*
> *Unites the world in song*

You still know nothing? (Gravesend, Britain: July 1871)

Death has wrought more blood on blood,
Civil war, and then invasion.
All of nature in a rage
Bent and twisted in convulsion.
I thirst for forceful hate,
For a storm on scale diluvian
But—O forest still so calm,
You still know nothing?

O, foolish calm, you sadden me.
I have seen cadavers trampled,
Piled up high on carts and wagons,
Dumped by executioners.
The quicklime and the blackened tomb

Will never share the number,
But here, with shining sky and dreamy swell,
You still know nothing?

In their thousands, freighter-prisons
Confine condemned and cursed by power.
These down-and-outs once fed their kin,
These convicts were fathers once,
Far away their pale-faced babes
Lack daily bread and die without.
But with buds still on your branches, O chestnut tree
You still know nothing?

And we cast ourselves in fire,
Artist, poet, laborer,
We hoped to move on up from here,
To pull humanity toward better fate.
But gangrene has seized our souls
And made us convicts, galley slaves.
What! Ashes only and no flame, volcano?
You still know nothing?

The ragged masses mowéd down,
Misery the fee,
What bread will we feed our daughters?
Our work, alas, what's to do?
We tried to give the most infirm,
The saving germ of citizenship.
But, O you Sun, empurpling peaks,
You still see nothing?

The drooling fang, the killing rage,
A hate-filled future frightens us.
The charnel house has drained our blood.
No more, no more, our hearts are dry.
France is stifled, suffocates,

Thanks to Prussians, Bourgeoisie.
What, magic fog, in wide blue yonder,
You still know nothing?

Saint Providence (1871)

Providence, an awful child,
Famine, war, revolt, and plague:
These her games grotesque and wild,
Provoked by whims, however vague.

Our melodrama her invention
And we her actors earn boos and frowns.
The traitor's knife that cuts us down,
Hers to plan with premeditation.

Fueled by shrapnel her crazy flights,
Thank her god after fights,
When human flesh has bled and bled.

Prudent people, guard your sphere,
For if you don't, you have to fear
That Providence will leave you shreds.

5: American Exile: 1873–80

Descending From the Cross (Boston 1875)

Seeing science make its début,
Jesus said: "I'll leave the cross.
I've served too long for pope and boss.
I'm not their lackey or their brute.

In your realm I cannot breathe,
A man of the people in the street
The Paris Commune made me meet.
I keep their faith with sword now sheathed.

And my apostles, idiots all,
Who have held too much in thrall.
Castrators all, they're people shredders.

Let me leave without these rogues,
For I can no longer act defender
I cannot play that stooge."

The Rotting Corpse (New York, 1875)

I saw a putrid rotting corpse,
A vessel of corrupting fumes,
For insects a natural source
Of food for a teaming horde.

Everybody gorged with pus,
Like a gourmet at a feast,
With fork in hand, face well stuffed,
I saw and parted from the beast.

But still surrounded by their stench,
The maggots their thirst did quench,
And yelled in chorus a single phrase:

Respect our sacred property!
Or do you want to undo the base
Of enduring society?

The Spider's Web (New York 1875)
To my friend Dr. Goupil, member of the Commune
[Freemason and chair of the committee that supported
Pottier in U.S. exile]

Slimy monster, sly and wild,
It extends so far it blocks our view.
This specter just grew and grew
To poison us, our lives defiled.

This parasite heeds no time nor place,
Makes the world a bank and nature seedy,
Sucks blood and brains of all the needy.
This spider monster is God and grace!

This specter whets our masters' claws,
From its throne disgorges laws
And priests that block our road ahead.

Take care you're not ensnared, ensnarled!
Shred the web that hooked the stars!
Drive out the spider and squash it dead!

The Workingmen of America to the Workingmen of France
(Newark, NJ; July 17, 1876)

To the delegates at large at the Centennial Exposition in Philadelphia in 1876 [and in anticipation of the Colonial Exposition that was to take place in Paris in 1878]. Title and italics in English

The social question to discuss,
Social problems to contend.
The International is all of us
Our task our differences to mend.
From your France or far beyond,
No more divided by the sea.
Welcome workers come to bond
And celebrate all labor's feats.

Artisans, name ambassadors,
Weavers, cobblers, foundry men,
Warmly greet and fill your glasses
To salute your friends again.
To elders who know the ropes,
And who sired the human race
And the youth with their new scopes
And other tools to speed the pace.

People to people, face to face,
Let us meet now in congress.
Labor must now change its pace
To push ahead our shared progress.
We must now act together,
Tracing a universal way
To fend off exploitation
And make the exploiters pay.

The government we must erase,
To our work it pays no mind.

The problem has a double face:
To us in rags the laws are blind
As they seize both yield and toil,
And attempt to smash our ties.
We should share our labor's fruit,
And build resources to secure our rise.

Offering us a questionnaire
When misery keeps us up at night
Is tantamount to giving bosses
The final word to solve our plight.
The night is dark, the times tumultuous,
It is dire, our situation.
For this reason, I'll take the podium
To speak about this Exposition.

I

Sure, a spectacle to inflate our pride.
The Exposition's magic spell.
Under grandiose iron frame, in the fairy garden,
Industries display their trophies.
The center holds the dizzying fire,
The growling steam-machine bests our tools,
With iron fists it crushes matter,
Armor-plates a dragon or extrudes a thread
Finer than any spider, spinning without end,
Padding for garments, tools, utensils,
Fill to bursting shops with goods.
Riches from the vaults to dazzle us,
Overflowing casks of gems,
Overstuffed, well-padded chairs,
Wrap body and soul in wadded cotton,
Plunge through bone-marrow to our deepest passions,
Refine the spice of prostitution,
Strip the women wrapped in gauze—

All sorted by country and displayed in cases.
This all is Philadelphia and will soon be Paris—
In just two years. Commerce schemes—but who pays the price?
The display cabinets of make-up products
Flirt and flatter passers-by. The barker barks and drums
And the public drunk on musk is taken in by spectacle.
Leering in, they cry: Oh Progress!

II

Progress! Really? Let us look more closely.
Industry, do you propose we judge you
   By the surface show?
You wrap yourself in blazing colors
But we who know the bloody rags beneath
   We will expose them!

For shame, the masses' empty bellies.
Their pale privation threatens
   Your stability
The poorest poor pay heaviest taxes.
Your perverted world falsely favors,
   Above all, property.

We will denounce your new Bastilles.
Your factories are no more than prisons,
   Which we ought to raze
And the inmates of these jails
Deprived of sun and country air
   Will you expose them?

The workers' food is full of maggots.
While your banquets stuff the guts
   Of the rich triumphant.
We must sell off piece by piece
Our worldly goods, as lack of work and hunger

Devour our children.

Luxury peddlers, in plain speech,
Tell us what debt we owe tuberculosis,
Tribute that heralds death!
Tell us with what contempt for life,
At three dollars a week, you destroy
    An adolescent's lungs!

Expose the limbs ground up by lathes,
The miners swallowed up by holes,
    And turned to coal!
The dead don't count in your charnel house,
Nor their abandoned families
    Live, if you only can!

Expose the *boss*, the boss of bosses,
Capitalist ruling as if divine,
    With no clue how to use a tool
Expose your tricks and your treason,
And the state that serves the master
    With a loaded gun!

In a paper, one of yours, we read of
Mammon slashing salaries
    Twenty percent.
The slave must yield when Master orders:
Workers: slit your wrists and shed your blood
    Twenty percent.

They will exploit panic and crisis;
From their decrees we can be sure
    They won't stop there.
You've sucked our blood; now, master, drink!
All this truth, not make-believe!
    Will you expose it?

Lying Liberty and bloody progress,
Machines are strong but people die.
   Even if the world is blind.
What point progress if we're off a cliff?
The point of product, if producers suffer?
   People matter more than trade!

III

Free trade and traffic, what a mess!
Dollars, francs, or piastres,
   Cash and cash the only goal!
These merchants make the world a shop,
Liberty! Republic! Shred your flags!
   Wrap yourselves within a shroud!

Do not endure the pirates' rule,
Reduce the gulf between the classes,
   Boss and worker.
But, with hard heads and soft hearts,
This era shoves us in the shit,
   This rotten century.

Yes, it's time to close the shop,
This shop of death, this shop of lies.
   Shut down the slaughter!
Shut down this joint where men are drowning
In absinthe and worse. To the curb,
   The cash collector!

Exploiter who cuts the world to his measure,
Bourgeois, usury is your name.
   It's an official disaster!
Expose the system and its agents,
The string-pullers, minions, and the millions
   In their hoard.

IV

Capitalist production
Driven by your hidden gears,
Rather than our social needs,
You're the buttress for the gallows!
For Johnny Misery, it's simply cruel
To snatch the bread right from his mouth,
While stuffing full the rich elites.

Bureaucracy is at your service.
The treadmills of the *status quo*,
Driven by the filthy rich.
Their inertia makes our misery.
All the hacks who spread their lies
For their bosses, bad customers.
Their paperwork fills barricades
That stymie progress and great works.

The saber-wielding cavalry,
The slayers of the Communards,
The beast that paws the ground and snorts,
The brute that pulls the plough:
Glorious they are not,
But you who would be rid of us,
Deploy an army to do your work,
And the hacks to bless your purge.

The Holy Church is at your service,
That incense peddler of old
Making a goodly profit
From charity for the poor
And all Christian souls.
For the glory of your God
You would convert Voltaire and the sages
Into sheep in holy pasture.

Press and P.R. serve you well.
You drug the public as do the priests.
Blackmail in pretty clothes
Peddling swindle mendaciously.
And your cynical accountants
Bankrupt nations and the poor,
Inflating paper money
While markets crash.

The legal system at your service
The courts collect and fleece the lost,
And condemn the down-and-outs,
While they acquit the well-to-do.
These old tribunals bend the law,
Subordinate justice to state,
Blow back and forth with politics,
And serve the rich and their ilk.

Police are at your service,
Always ready to crush heads,
While Capital still robs us blind,
We're the ones caught in the net.
In the police inventory
They hold at ready the sharpest tool,
Spreading rumors of conspiracy
To justify their bloody force.

Republican or monarchist
Whatever else the liberals say
About the ragged, rumpled mob
They still pump us full of lead.
To ensure the rich stay rich
And accumulate all capital,
You'll entrap the world in nets,
And deliver it to Caesar's lair.

High above the living world
You suspend a bogeyman:
The *Boss* takes a break from his affairs,
After a good week's haul,
To deliver rebels to the flames
—Hell is merely your decor—
And your good Lord squashes souls
As your executioner does us.

V

All in place, the apparatus:
Media, courts, and jails and banks,
From pope to rug-rat at your service.
The financier that denies our due—
He pays artists, scholars, and the workers—
All producers—and signs their work.
Monopolists will crush us all.
What to do, proletariat?
We improvise but he moves the world,
Blasts an island, gouges out the Alps.
Digs canals under the sea.
Big capital acts and struts,
Drops his millions from dizzy heights.
He owns the globe and can toss it out,
Holds life itself in deathly squeeze.
And we, the workers, in misery's mire!
Misery bears down and crushes us,
Sucks our blood, our sweat, our tears,
Vice and press will crush us dead.
        Is this not enough?

Yes! If we rise up and act as one
Poverty gets no more blood.
We exceed the rich a hundred-fold.
Our loss if we let them suck us dry.

VI

Commune! Where have you gone?
Where the red flag and the ardent hearts?
Fight the monster, arise, arise!
Complete the task and play your part!

The Communal program, it's yours, my friend!
Tell the idle not to shirk,
Make the workshops hum again,
Restore the world to those who work.

And reunite after wretched years,
In this centennial all as one
All for the goal of Humanity
For the universe, a new Commune!

Marguerite
To his daughter Marguerite Petit (South Boston 1877)

Marguerite is five years old, and free
Of baptism or another rite.
Birds sing to her, the sun is bright,
And kiss her with joy and glee.

Birdsong is her daily rite.
She likes the sky, the flame, the light,
And clouds that cross at window height.
Your red flag, Commune, is her delight.

Without the Church her Sundays lead
To fragile buds on the trees.
Nature guides her budding mind.

In this great world she seeks for sense.

A blooming cabbage inspires intense
Attention: "look at it laugh!"

Matter not the Bible (Boston, 1877)

Oh Matter! Simple bodies that with ease arise,
Whirlwinds endlessly entwined,
A cycle that the source refines,
The furnace that with love allies.

The atom at the core of all,
The universe and human mind
Will not yield to creed or thrall.
On this point, our Bible finds:

Almighty naught that floats on water
For all eternity—'til God the idler
One fine day felt creation's urge.

The stage is set for trickster's games,
Conjuring creation in the flames
Now here, now gone, on the verge.

The phases of equality (Paterson, NJ 1878)
To citizen Berthe P.

Tell us, O Past, your gloomy tales
Of pharaohs' brutal yokes.
Humans marching in the dark
Leave behind a trail of blood.
But the day will dawn, the east light up.
Raise your eyes to rays and note:
Slave and master the same at source.
    Arise, arise! Equality is here!

Luther rose and Caesar fell,
The press knocked down the feudal keep.
Before the law, equality stands firm,
From day to day expand ideals.
Enlightenment rebuts the Church,
God up in smoke, and humanity unchained.
Free-thinking faith in human rights alone
    Arise! Arise! Equality is here!

But usurers still rule the earth,
And bigger fish still swallow small.
Tired of suffering, at last the proles
Settle debts and pick up tools.
Labor rules and harvest's great.
In justice and majesty
Workers will share the yield.
    Arise! Arise! Equality is here!

The Commune Came Through Here (Paterson, NJ. 1879)
To Edouard Vaillant, member of the Commune

The Commune is a thunder shock,
And Paris can be proud.
This unsettled globe smells powder,
Everything as yesterday.
Defeat awaiting its revenge:
Fracasse, Vautour, Loyola
All now on shaky ground.
    The Commune came through here.

The fight has pulled up pavement stone,
Decimated battalions.
Equality has steered the plough
Through the furrow's deepest trough.
A massacre immense it was,

But everywhere where blood flowed down
We see the germinating seed.
   The Commune came through here.

The Commune loathed the fake big man,
Planted on the plinth up high,
And his cult of war:
An insult to humanity
Let Chauvin howl or scandalmonger,
The rearguard monkey for Attila
Has fallen at a finger snap
   The Commune came through here.

He reminds you of the Tuileries,
And the December executioner,
Turned by jokes and dirty tricks,
A Big Number, wholesale slaughter.
And this time of plague and lucre
He gives to love the note, the la.
One day they will sweat it out.
   The Commune came through here.

United States and ancient Europe,
United Labor has its congress.
Science has prepared the fire
And our hammers will forge progress.
In the light of day our future rolls,
No borders will block its way.
All people have but one program:
   The Commune came through here.

Our Congress declares and we assert
The earth, the mines, the pits, canal, and rail,
Steamer, factory, telegraph,
All great instruments of work
For production on the grandest scale.

Let everything be socialized!
Let us expunge the idle class!
  The Commune came through here.

Our brains absorb the shining light,
Which makes all workers grow,
In workshops, cottages,
Better trained and living better.
Even from most humble hovels
They cry, the great day has come,
As the red flag fills their dreams:
  The Commune came through here!

The Age of the World (Paterson, NJ 1880)

A hundred thousand years is not that much
For planets—is our world that old?
Yes, say geologists. And what says Loyola?
Scripture, Puritans, the bible's word?

However old, the globe has woes:
The pope, the plague, famine, war
The bankers have us all in thrall
But humanity will fight these lows.

Will you still speak, silly goose
Of ogres and the good Lord's tales
Of Eden and of fallen Man?

Even if we fear the world's end,
The globe's corn-golden hair, touched
By its sun ancestor, saying "welcome, child."

6: Return to the Third Republic (1881–87)

Johnny Misery [Jean Misère] (1881)
> *Pottier introduced the character* Johnny Misery *[Jean
> Misère] in the long exile poem* The Workingmen of America
> to the Workingmen of France, *but this ballad was written
> shortly after he returned to Paris from U.S. exile. It was
> published as a pamphlet* Jean Misère *(Paris: Oriol, 1883)
> and in* Chants Révolutionnaires *(1887). Despite—or
> perhaps because of—its gloomy outlook on the difficult lives
> of returning exiles, it became a popular song, reprinted
> several times after Pottier's death.*

In tattered coat, just skin and bone,
Fever-ravaged, at a loss,
Johnny Misery cries his own,
"Misery, you're the boss."
   And yet—
What in the end will we get?

"No star in sight, and no friend!
The world a desert, parched the veld.
If it burned, I'd go up in flames.
If it rains, I may just melt."
   And yet—
What in the end will we get?

My writing pad, is this the end?
No holiday, no meager pay
Not the strength even to defend
My wretched life another day.
   And yet—
What in the end will we get?

I was once, in days gone by,
A decent tailor, but now I'm old.

A rag, a wreck, about to die,
But the workers' story must be told.
   And yet—
What in the end will we get?

Since time began, bad pay, no rest.
But we must take it, or we die.
Machines to them we are at best,
We cannot strike, we cannot lie.
   When will this all end?

This is the lesson of the rich:
They preach the faith of kith and kin,
But their war left my son in a ditch
Their lust and money bought my daughter's skin.
   And yet—
What in the end will we get?

The holy church will bless their loot,
And these callous and rapacious thieves
And when our goods enrich the brutes
Their dear God will give them leave.
   And yet—
What in the end will we get?

One day, the heavens were aglow,
And the sunshine lit my rags.
I grabbed a gun for the National Guard
And raised the people's scarlet flag.
   And yet—
What in the end will we get?

In our thousands, we crouched down deep,
The gloomy dark lit by the moon
When someone pulled me from the heap,
I shouted: *Vive la Commune!*

And yet—
What in the end will we get?

Farewell, the martyrs of this war,
Farewell, those locked in prison damp.
Will we die on foreign shore?
Or will we endure and escape the camp?
  And yet—
What in the end will we get?

Political Economy (Paris 1881)
To the Professors at the Collège de France

Of all the rights of humanity
The most legitimate of them all
Is commercial liberty:
Capital's right to hold in thrall.
The laws of supply, demand
While morality goes up in smoke.
You must buy, you must sell.
All trade is free. Laissez-faire!

And nothing more can shock the rich
As they dispense their poison pill.
If the merchant inflates his sales
Success rewards him as we fall.
Whether mustard, morphine,
Or more commodities,
Selling, buying and more schemes.
All trade is free. Laissez-faire!

Workers resist this financial gain.
Wise men cannot keep them tame.
It's time again to cut their pay,
Push profits up, keep costs at bay,

By cutting wages by the hour,
Millions will take a hit.
Do you think that some will die?
Laissez-faire! All trade is free.

The market for our wares in vogue
Will offer the best returns.
Pay no mind to demagogues,
Who predict a glut and adverse terms.
What we need despite mistakes
Is work, work, work at breakneck speed,
To inundate the marketplace.
Laissez-faire! All trade is free.

For our workers' full well-being
Let's them all work double-time.
Bring in women, children, all to slave
In factories—a cruel crime.
Neglect your kids and your homes.
Come work for us—and when you're done,
You get unemployment, off you go!
All trade is free. Laissez-faire!

Monopolize all the food,
Shut up shop and dock and say goodbye,
Split bad workers from the good
To restrict labor supply
As for the victims, stop your laments
Those we crush and those we fleece
Economic maxims the law cements:
Laissez-faire! All trade is free.

First published as "Laissez-faire, laissez-passer", *Poésies d'écono-mie sociale* (Paris: Oriol, 1884)

The Holy Trinity (Paris 1882)
To Hovelaque, city counselor

First: Religion: the gargoyle of old
Who deceives the naive with dogmatic must,
Who keeps the people kneeling, cold,
Sells them miracles and leaves them dust.

Property: furniture or land—
Declares: is I that gives you work
But the sales pitch yields only sand.
The bourgeois leave us in the murk.

And then there's *order:* general, Caesar.
Bless the slaughter to keep the peace.
We must fight; they won't risk a hair.

Priest, banker, hired gun—three in one,
Holy trinity—hold us ransom.
Deceit, theft and murder, all your heirs.

Out of work, out of wood (Paris 1884)
To Léon Cladel

My boss has no work for us,
And we are out of wood.
It's winter and forced idleness
Will destroy us well and good.

Not even work for fleas.
It's snowing; skies are grey.
At every shop I knock to see.
I've been searching every day.
Nothing to sell, no credit yet,
And the rent we must pay.

Everywhere I'm told to wait,
But hunger will not delay.

Oh, the rich (may God forgive them)
Have told me often: "my friend:
When employed, look out ahead.
Act like the ant and do not spend."
Save! But we live from wage to wage.
We hardly have enough to eat.
At fortnight's end we're out again
And may be forced onto the street.

The nights are hard in our tenement.
No more soup to keep us warm.
With no more to show than sentiment
Mother in rags must heed the storm.
Her children must all shiver and freeze
Every night from dusk to dawn.
Their bedclothes and breeches
Must go—again—to be pawned.

And last winter, my heart's still sore,
We lost our youngest to the cold.
It's a rare child that survives at all,
And mothers struggle the rest to hold.
As winter comes, as harsh as ever,
I fear the twins may go in turn.
The dead may well be gone forever,
But those behind must grieve and yearn.

How many weighed down with all this woe
Drink themselves into a daze?
Meanwhile, there's my eldest girl
I fear I may not see her raised.
A sixteen-year-old may attend a ball,
If God allows her to pay her way!

But, if she's poor, no chance at all.
We can't afford to make her day.

I can't take much more as I go
Across the bridge home at night,
I hear the water sigh and groan,
And speak to me of my own plight.
Do you mourn humanity,
Old river, in your depths so black?
As you echo widows' plaints
And sobbing orphans in their shack.

My boss has no work for us,
And we are out of wood.
It's winter and forced idleness
Will destroy us well and good.

The Monument for the Commune Dead (1883)

[The French title—*Le Monument des fédérés*—refers
to the National Guard but the poem evidently honors
all Commune defenders.]

To Alphonse Humbert, city counselor (May 1883)

On this spot the butchers came
In Bloody Week to dump our dead
In a ditch right near this wall.
They could not know our names would spread.
Thirteen years ago, my friends,
Paris rests and makes amends.
  Let barricades be raised.
  The National Guard is to be praised.

Our monument of simple stone

Rough-hewn and with ivy spread.
The Academy can paint their own
But we remember the people's dead.
From Delescluze, the oldest and the first,
To women, children, their bodies burst.
  Let the Commune rise again.
  The Commune's monument: a world to gain.

As we bear witness, the bourgeois reign,
Strip away our work and make us starve,
Thrash our kin with toil that kills and maims,
As profits rise and not by halves.
And when we pile up against the wall,
They stuff their faces and take it all.
  Let the Commune's monument damn their deeds.
  The prosecution rests its case; let the judge proceed.

Published as a chapbook signed: *Eugène Pottier, former Communard* (Paris: A. Derrine, 1884)

To Each His Trade (1883)
  To the tune of: J'ai vu la Meunière.

  Silver Medal Winner at the *Lice chansonnier*
  (Song Competition). Paris, August 1883

An undertaker, as he drank a drop,
  Said aside to the cop:
Drudgery won't get you far,
Much beyond the funeral car.
With six to feed, dear Thomas, I
Have not enough to get by.
  Death won't get us far!
  Death won't do at all!

God knows that a poisoned spring
  Would bring us just a little trade—
For me, apothecaries,
  And the quacks.
Lead coffins, marble tombs, silk trim,
Death's a living, however grim.
  Death won't get us far!
  Death won't do at all!

In this cemetery
  The common grave is packed.
But the worker's misery
  Still endures. Fact.
Hospitals supply dead in heaps,
And our sweethearts only weep.
  Death won't get us far!
  Death won't do at all!

Death, it's true, leaves in the lurch,
  All of us upon this earth,
But what to do? It is our work.
  We make a living from the scourge.
  Death won't get us far!
  Death won't do at all!

Simple Counsel (1884)

First published in *Poésies de l'Economie sociale* (1884)

Is science a mere illusion?
Like the cross that spreads delusion?
Must we believe or stop exclusion?
  Look!

The weighty state rests on deceit,

On misdeeds, taxes, and the cheat.
Is it time a better world to greet?
  Act!

The banker's graft rests on the law,
Swallows our goods in his maw.
When will he our wealth restore?
  Seize!

The Commune did not die (Paris; May 1886)
  To the survivors of Bloody Week [May 1871]

Killed by rifle shots,
Or machine-gun fire,
Wrapped in her flag
In clayish earth.
The fat butcher's mob
Thought itself on top.
But this won't stop us saying:
  The Commune did not die!

Just as reapers raze a field,
Just as pears fall to earth,
The *Versaillais* came to slaughter
One hundred thousand at very least
And these a hundred thousand dead
You will see what they can tell.
But this won't stop us saying:
  The Commune did not die!

Yes, they shot Varlin,
Flourens, Duval, Millière,
Ferré, Rigault, Tony Moilin.
But enough of counting dead—
They thought they could sever limbs

And drain our blood
But this won't stop us saying:
    The Commune did not die!

They behaved like crafty thieves,
Sneaking silently around,
Killing wounded in their beds,
Even in the ambulances.
And the blood soaked through the sheets,
Seeped and flowed under the doors.
But this won't stop us saying:
    The Commune did not die!

Journalists and the police
Smear their lies and defamation,
Spreading on our charnel houses
Waves of misinformation
Maxime Du Camp, and the Dumas
May vomit up their boozy lies,
But this won't stop us saying:
    The Commune did not die!

It's the sword of Damocles
That hangs above their heads
The funeral of Jules Vallès
Made them act with stupid dread,
Facing our waves of men
Serving as Vallès's escort
Those men prove in any case:
    The Commune did not die!

In short, this proves to those who fought
That our Marianne is well tanned
And that it's time to shout
Vive la Commune yet again!
And it proves to every Judas

That this is how it goes
And that they will see soon that
  The Commune did not die!

This poem was the final entry in Chants révolutionnaires
*(1887) The compilers, Pottier's Communard colleagues, editor
Jean Allemanne, writers Henri Rochefort and Jules Vallès, and
singer-songwriter Gustave Nadaud evidently hoped that the
Commune and those who died on the barricades—Eugène Varlin,
Gustave Flourens, Emile Duval, Jean-Baptiste Millière, Théophile
Ferré, Raoul Rigault—would inspire other revolutionaries in
France and beyond.*

The Hidden Wall (Paris, May 1886)
  To Séverine Vingtras who inspired this poem

  *Bourgeoisie, your history
  Is written on this wall.
  History, not obscure memory,
  Trumps your mean hypocrisy.*

Here it stands, atop our bones,
This massive grave for the dead of May.
Over all the years, we recall the day,
And the dead beneath the stones.
Here, the plundered workers lie.
In this hole, the unknown dead
Beneath this wall once stained with blood:
They bear witness to your crimes!

Adolphe Thiers and his clique
Sprayed these old bricks with your blood.
They dragged your names through the mud.
But in time the truth will speak.
In this once darkened ground,

Truth will count the martyred dead,
And your history will be read;
And your praises will resound.

The rich are laid in marble tombs,
Their crypts are garnished with their greed,
An insult to our tattered weeds
And our mourners in the gloom.
Such a contrast mocks our grief,
Our stony ground lacks trees and grass,
Their tombs have shining pearls and brass,
Ours obscured, deflect belief.

You who never quenched your taste
For our flesh you used to shred.
Even sunshine you deny our dead,
Just as in life, their names defaced.
You built a church to hide our deeds,
Your monuments obscure our graves,
No flowers granted to mere slaves,
No sunshine to nourish seed.

Counting all the working class
How many—women, children, aged men—
Mowed down by your machine guns
Mercenaries turned on us *en masse*.
What's our choice: to live like slaves?
To fight for dignity and bread,
Fight until we drop down dead?
And then they still deny us graves!

But indignation's on the rise,
The people are no longer blind,
We know our martyrs lie behind
The Communal wall you tried to hide.
A wind is blowing through the land,

The sun will rise to our high noon,
The masses join the new Commune,
And turn bloody shrouds into red flags.

> *Bourgeoisie, your history*
> *Is written on this wall.*
> *History, not obscure memory,*
> *Trumps your mean hypocrisy.*

Anniversary of March 18, 1871 (1887)

> *Our misery may be dark and long,*
> *But comrades we must still unite,*
> *Raise our glasses, hearts in song,*
> *Celebrate Communal fight.*

On this day still unafraid
Escaping the hidden snare
Flagstones recall the barricades,
The trembling sun the whole affair.
Let us revive the Commune's call,
Unique in History despite its fall,
And for the future we seek one day
March 18th will show the way.

This was the day of unknown men
And women who played their parts,
Shirtless ones who rose again,
Their names a trace on our ramparts.
Proletarian they may have been,
But armed with solidarity
And equality, still strove to win
Against the Versaillais MPs.

City Hall our meeting place,

Where we gathered to proclaim
And Paris did us embrace,
And the Commune earned its fame.
The cannon thundered wake-up calls
To defeat the bourgeoisie
Under the sun teemed one and all
Waxing in solidarity.

It was a radiant day in that spring,
A *Germinal* to spur our growth.
The Red Flag moved us all to sing,
To revolution a solemn oath.
The flag embellished all our rags,
The sun above sent down its rays,
To honor even miners' slag
Dispel the darkness, raise our gaze.

> *Our misery may be dark and long,*
> *But comrades, we must still unite,*
> *Raise our glasses, hearts in song,*
> *Celebrate Communal fight.*

L'internationale marche

Parole E. Pottier   Musique P. Degeyter

chant avec Piano

Déposé Pour tous Pays

Par Pierre Degeyter

fait a Lille en 1888

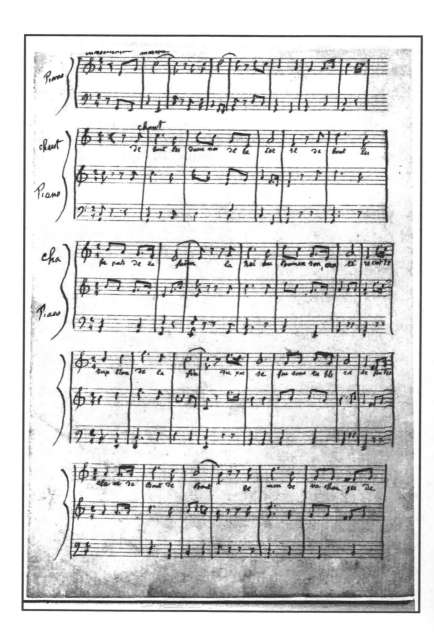

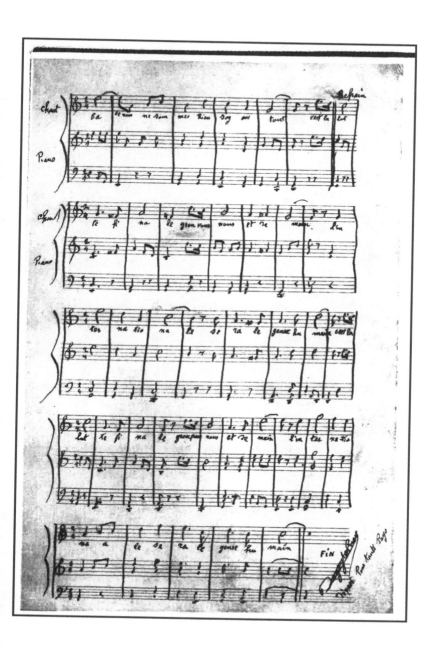

PART 3: L'INTERNATIONALE: FRENCH ORIGINAL AND ENGLISH VERSIONS

Eugène Pottier wrote the *Internationale* after the fall of the Paris Commune at the end of May 1871. It appeared in his *Chants révolutionnaires*, published in April 1887, before his death in November. Like several of his earlier revolutionary songs, it was initially sung to the tune of *La Marseillaise*, which has been the French republican anthem since 1793. Pierre Degeyter's setting, which is today the usual but not the only accompaniment, was improvised on the harmonium by Degeyter for workers participating in the *Lyre des Travailleurs* in 1888, after Pottier's death in 1887.

This section reprints the French text published in 1887 followed by English-language versions in chronological order. I have added short prefaces about the origin or publication record of each. For versions in other languages and my translations, see Part 4.

L' Internationale (May 1871)
  A Gustave Lefrançais, Communard

Pottier's text begins with the refrain rather than the first verse.

C'est la lutte finale
Groupons-nous et demain

L'Internationale
Sera le genre humain.

Debout! les damnés de la terre
Debout! les forçats de la faim
La raison tonne en son cratère,
C'est l'éruption de la fin.
Du passé faisons table rase
Foule esclave, debout! debout!
Le monde va changer de base
Nous ne sommes rien, soyons tout!

Refrain (x2)
C'est la lutte finale
Groupons-nous et demain
L'Internationale
Sera le genre humain.

Il n'est pas de sauveurs suprêmes:
Ni dieu, ni césar, ni tribun,
Producteurs, sauvons-nous nous-mêmes!
Décrétons le salut commun!
Pour que le voleur rende gorge,
Pour tirer l'esprit du cachot
Soufflons nous-mêmes notre forge
Battons le fer quand il est chaud!

Refrain (x2)

L'etat opprime et la loi triche,
L'impôt saigne le malheureux,
Nul devoir ne s'impose au riche,
Le droit du pauvre est un mot creux.
C'est assez languir en tutelle,
L'égalité veut d'autres lois;
«Pas de droits sans devoirs», dit-elle,
«Egaux, pas de devoirs sans droits!»

Refrain (x2)

Hideux dans leur apothéose,
Les rois de la mine et du rail
Ont-ils jamais fait autre chose
Que dévaliser le travail?
Dans les coffres-forts de la bande
Ce qu'il a créé s'est fondu.
En décrétant qu'on le lui rende
Le peuple ne veut que son dû.

Refrain (x2)

Les rois nous saoulaient de fumées.
Paix entre nous, guerre aux tyrans!
Appliquons la grève aux armées,
Crosse en l'air et rompons les rangs!
S'ils s'obstinent, ces cannibales,
A faire de nous des héros,
Ils sauront bientôt que nos balles
Sont pour nos propres généraux.

Refrain (x2)

Ouvriers, paysans, nous sommes
Le grand parti des travailleurs;
La terre n'appartient qu'aux hommes,
L'oisif ira loger ailleurs.
Combien de nos chairs se repaissent!
Mais si les corbeaux, les vautours,
Un de ces matins disparaissent,
Le soleil brillera toujours!

Refrain

First English translation (1871)

Version attributed to Pottier during his brief stay in
Gravesend in England, before he sailed for the United
States (*www.marxists.org*). Sung by, among others,
English balladeer Ewan McColl (James Henry Miller,
1915–86), who, as American readers may know, was
married to Peggy Seeger.

Arise ye workers from your slumbers
Arise ye prisoners of want
For reason in revolt now thunders
And at last ends the age of cant.
Away with all your superstitions
Servile masses arise, arise
We'll change henceforth the old tradition
And spurn the dust to win the prize.

> *Refrain (x2)*
> *So, comrades, come rally,*
> *And the last fight let us face.*
> *The Internationale*
> *Unites the human race.*

No more deluded by reaction
On tyrants only we'll make war
The soldiers too will take strike action
They'll break ranks and fight no more
And if those cannibals keep trying
To sacrifice us to their pride,
They soon shall hear the bullets flying
We'll shoot the generals on our own side.

> *Refrain (x2)*

No saviour from on high delivers,

No faith have we in prince or peer.
Our own right hand the chains must shiver
Chains of hatred, greed and fear.
E'er the thieves will out with their booty
And give to all a happier lot,
Each at the forge must do their duty,
And we'll strike while the iron is hot.

Refrain (x2)

American Translation by Charles H. Kerr, publisher (1894)

This version appeared in the *IWW Songbook* (Chicago: Charles H. Kerr, 1909) and in subsequent editions of this anthology.

Arise, ye prisoners of starvation!
Arise, ye wretched of the earth,
For justice thunders its condemnation,
A better world's in birth.
No more tradition's chains will bind us,
Arise, ye slaves, no more in thrall!
The earth will rise on new foundations,
We have been naught; we shall be all.

Refrain (x2)
'Tis the final conflict,
Let each stand in place,
The Internationale
Shall be the human race.

We want no condescending saviors
To rule us from a judgement hall;
We workers ask not for their favors;
Let us consult for all.

To make the thief disgorge his booty
To free the spirit from its cell,
We must ourselves decide our duty,
We must decide and do it well.

Refrain (x2)

Behold them seated in their glory,
The kings of mine and rail and soil!
What have you read in all their story.
But how they plundered toil?
Fruits of the workers' toil are buried
In the strong coffers of a few;
In working for their restitution
The men will only ask their due.

Refrain (x2)

Toilers from all fields united
Join hand in hand with all who work;
The earth belongs to us, the workers,
No room here for the shirk.
How many on our flesh have fattened!
But if the vicious birds of prey
Shall vanish from the sky some morning
The blessed sunlight then will stay.

Refrain (x2)

The International Marching Song of the Revolutionary Proletariat (New York: Labor News Co., 1911, under the auspices of the (U.S.) Socialist Labor Party, led by Daniel DeLeon.

Stand up! Ye wretched ones who labor,
Stand up! Ye galley-slaves of want.
Man's reason thunders from its crater,
'Tis th' eruption naught can daunt.
Of the past let us cleanse the tables,
Mass enslaved, fling back the call,
Old Earth is changing her foundations,
We have been nothing, now be all.

> *Refrain (x2)*
> *'Tis the last call to battle!**
> *Close the ranks, each in place,*
> *The staunch old International*
> *Shall be the Human race.*

There are no saviors e'er will help us,
Nor God, nor Caesar, nor Tribune,
'Tis ours, O workers, must the blows be
That shall win the common boon.
From the thief to wring his stolen booty,
From its prison to free the soul.
'Tis we ourselves must ply the bellows,
'Tis we must beat the anvil's roll.

> *Refrain (x2)*

The state is false, the law's a mockery,
And exploitation bows us down;
The rich man flaunts without a duty,
And the poor man's rights are none.
Long enough have we in swaddling languished,

Lo, Equality's new law
"Away with rights that know no duties,
Away with duties shorn of rights."

Refrain (x2)

All hideous in their brutal lordship
Stand king of mill and mine and rail.
When have they e'er performed a service,
Or at work done aught but quail?
In the coffers of these robber barons,
Blind the world's great wealth is thrown,
In summ'ning them to restitution,
The people seeks but what's its own.

Refrain (x2)

Toilers from shop and field united,
The Party we of all who work;
The earth belongs to those who labor,
Hence! the idler and the shirk!
Say, how many on our flesh have feasted?
But if all this vampire flight
Should vanish from the sky some morning,
The sun will still shine on us as bright!

Refrain

www.marxists.org attributes an alternative first line to the
refrain—*'Tis the last cause to battle*—to Helen Keller in a 1919
letter to Eugene Debs, formerly Socialist Party candidate for
U.S. president.

Jamaican Workers Party (1978–92)

Arise, ye toilers of all nations,
Condemned to misery and woe.
To hell with humbleness and patience,
Give deadly battle to the foe.

> *Refrain (x2)*
> *Proletarians, come rally,*
> *And the last fight let us face.*
> *The Internationale*
> *Unites the human race.*

No God, no king, no politician
Will win for us a better day.
So let us drop the old traditions,
Forge weapons for the coming fray.

> *Refrain*

Recording identified as Jamaican reggae but sounds
more like ska.
https://www.youtube.com/watch?v=D0uBuO4mXz0

The Internationale (adapted by singer-songwriter
Billy Bragg, 1990)

In an interview accompanying *We Began to Sing*, a record
tribute to Pete Seeger on May 3, 2020, Bragg recalled that
he wrote the first verse in response to a prompt from Seeger
at a concert to commemorate the activists of Tiananmen
Square in 1989. Since he did not like the nineteenth
century British version and knew no French, Bragg wrote
the verse based on Seeger's rough translation of the French.
After the fall of the Berlin Wall and prompted by his sense

in 1990 that the whole legacy of the left risked being tossed onto the trash heap of history along with the collapsing Communist bloc, he produced a version that appealed to international solidarity in more ecumenical language than the original militant ballad.

Stand up, all victims of oppression,
For tyrants fear your might.
Don't cling so hard to your possessions,
You have nothing if you have no rights.
Let racist ignorance be ended,
For respect makes empires fall,
Freedom merely privilege extended,
Unless enjoyed by one and all.

> *Refrain*
> *So, come brothers and sisters,*
> *For the struggle carries on.*
> *The Internationale*
> *Unites the world in song.*
> *So, comrades come rally*
> *For this is the time and place*
> *The Internationale*
> *Unites the human race.*

Let no-one build walls to divide us,
Walls of hatred or walls of stone.
Come greet the dawn and stand beside us,
We'll live together or die alone.
In our world poisoned by exploitation,
Those who have taken, now they must give,
And end the vanity of nations.
We've but one world on which to live.

> *Refrain*

And so begins the final drama
In the streets and in the fields.
We stand unbowed before their armour,
We defy their guns and shields.
When we fight provoked by their aggression,
Let us be inspired by like and love.
For though they offer us concessions,
Change will not come from above.

Refrain

Billy Bragg, *The Internationale* in *We Began to Sing: Celebrating Pete Seeger's Legacy*, May 3, 2020: *https://www.songkeepers.ca*

For Billy Bragg's comments on the origin of his version, see: https://www.youtube.com/watch?v=NBgfNy7dk4I

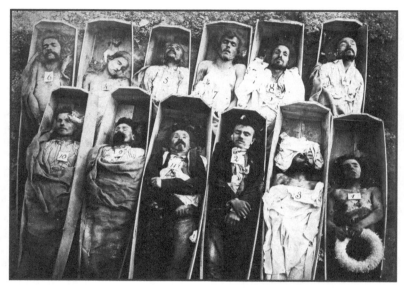

Communards Killed During Bloody Week, May 1871.
Photograph by Eugène Disdéri. Courtesy of the
Bibliothèque Nationale, Paris

PART 4: THE INTERNATIONALE FROM AFRIKAANS TO ZULU

The Internationale has appeared in print or in recordings in about eighty languages worldwide. Many of these versions, especially those in regional variations of world languages, such as Spanish, reflect distinct historical conditions and aspirations. As indicated in the introduction, my translation attempts to convey the meaning of the whole text and its context, rather than the more limited target of the word, the line, or even the verse. Local versions of political songs are more compelling if they respond to the conditions and aspirations of the target users, activists, and audiences, than if they merely attempt to reproduce line-by-line equivalence of the original text. My translations therefore attempt to convey the distinct image and melodic repertoire available to source speakers while also producing English versions that lend themselves to song or recitation.

These versions were produced for marches and other political assemblies; they rarely include the names of the translator or the singers, solo or in chorus. The scarcity of this information is nonetheless instructive because it reminds us that the mode of transmission of the *Internationale,* has been mostly oral and collective rather than, with some notable exceptions, the individual creation of a writer aiming for publication. The demands of transmitting an effective marching song produce variations within languages, variations that sometimes reflect regional, sometimes ideological, differences, or both.

I have organized this section alphabetically by language. I begin with Afrikaans: this striking post-apartheid version draws attention not only to the long history of the Communist Party of South Africa (est. 1922) but also to the transnational links among South African leftists, the Soviet Union, and its allies through 1990, and socialists in today's global South. Despite the apartheid government's obsession with making Afrikaans racially pure, speakers of Afrikaans, which was created in the seventeenth and eighteenth century by enslaved people's responses to Malay and Portuguese as well as to the Dutch spoken at the Cape of Good Hope, have been brown, black, and white. The version from Belgian Wallonia, the (more or less) French-speaking industrial region of southern Belgium, is best described as Belgian to place it geographically and to highlight the dialect that distinguishes it from Pottier's French. Since the Flemish version in use in northern Belgium differs only slightly from the Dutch, I have added a brief note on Flemish after the Dutch version.

The difference between the two German versions has in contrast nothing to do with dialect. The split between the Socialist Second International, founded by Marx's collaborator Friedrich Engels in the 1880s, and the German Communist Party, founded in 1919 by Karl Liebknecht and Rosa Luxemburg in response to the Bolshevist Revolution of 1917, did not immediately prompt a new version. Communist poet Erich Weinert wrote his version in 1929, at a time when Moscow's dismissal of the German Socialist Party as "social fascists" split the left opposition to the Nazis, who came to power in 1933. Despite the date of composition, the milder language of Weinert's version appears to reflect the broader Popular Front against Fascism of the 1930s, at which time Weinert was in exile in the Soviet Union. Weinert's version returned with him to East Germany and was the standard version in the German Democratic Republic (GDR: 1949–89), where it was reprinted in a centennial edition with woodcuts by Frans Masreel in 1971. The Dutch version appears to have borrowed elements from Luckhardt's German as well as from the original French. The Yiddish version, despite the linguistic proximity between Yiddish and German, appears to take as its point of departure the Russian version by Arkady Yakovievich Kots (1902); Kots was born to a Jewish family in Odesa, who may have known Yiddish. While faithful to the *Internationale*'s secular message of revolutionary transformation of existing society, the Yiddish version nonetheless includes Hebrew words that might be identified as *loshn-koydesh* [sacred language]; for instance, this version calls the coming new world a Gan-Ayden or "garden of Eden" and uses *memshala* which denotes divine governance, to characterize workers' future dominion over the world.

Spanish has the largest number of variants, Iberian and Latin American, which reflect ideological as well as regional differences. The rival versions in Castilian Spanish respond to disputes between socialists and anarchists in the Second Spanish Republic (1931–39) and the civil war (1936–39), and sharpen the contrast between the worldwide aspirations of the Socialist International and the Iberian Anarchist Federation (est. 1927). The differences among versions in Latin America, by contrast, do not clearly follow ideological fault lines. The version currently on the Cuban government site, for instance, uses notably less militant language than a 1980s Colombian guerrilla version that its users attribute to the Cuban revolution of 1959. In Portuguese, the differences between the Brazilian and peninsular versions are more subtle than the Spanish but still significant. The Brazilian version dates from the brief communist revolution of 1930 and omits the critique of kings that appears in the original French and in the peninsular Portuguese version, even though the latter is more recent, dating from the death of long-time dictator António de Oliveira Salazar in 1970.

Across the southern hemisphere from Latin America, the South African versions in Afrikaans and Zulu highlight the legacies of the South African left. The Communist Party of

South Africa, as it was then known, was founded in 1922 and recruited workers and intellectuals whatever their home language or ethnicity. Even unions and other leftist organizations that broke with the CPSA, such as the Garment Workers Union, were racially integrated until the 1950s, and signaled their integration by singing the *Internationale*. Despite its allegiance to the Moscow line in the 1930s, the CPSA was the only South African political party in the era of segregation— until it was suppressed in 1950—to consistently promote the education and advancement of black people. The party sponsored many who showed leadership potential for study in the USSR, such as James La Guma and his son Alex La Guma who published an account of his travels in the Soviet Union which highlighted the Caucasian and Central Asian republics. These connections allowed the party, after the CPSA was banned by the apartheid government (1950–1990), to reorganize in exile as the South African Communist Party (SACP), and to exercise significant influence on the African National Congress during these years.

The Zulu version of the *Internationale* was sung by the SACP in exile and in country by returning exiles and new recruits to the rehabilitated party after 1990. Even if the SACP has lost ground in the 21st century to the left-populist Economic Freedom Front (EFF), the Zulu version of the song still merits attention because it conveys an internationalist message using distinctive African figures of speech that highlight local interpretations of international solidarity. It suggests that the new world will ripen like cultivated crops and, in the refrain, that the international movement shapes human beings like the clay habitually used to make cooking pots and other everyday vessels. The Afrikaans version reprinted here is, however, a more recent version from 2013, by singer Liela Groenewald. I have included it because Groenewald changes the refrain from the British one familiar also to South Africans—"Comrades, come rally"—to "Skouer aan skouer *in die suide*" ("Shoulder to shoulder *in the South*"; emphasis added), which reminds singers and audience of Afrikaans's creole history and links this version to twenty-first century networks of solidarity and to the critical view of the world from the global South.

Afrikaans (Liela Groenewald, 2013)

Staan op verworpes van die wêreld	Stand up, all outcasts of the world!
Staan op uit boeie van jou waan	Shake off delusion's chain!
So magtig dreun die stem van rede	The voice of reason will roar in force
En 'n nuwe dag breek an	And a new day will dawn.
Ons boesems buig voor geen geloof meer	Our breasts will bow to no religion,
Ons baar geen slawe van die kerk	We dismiss the servants of the church.
Ons staan nou enig en berade	We stand firm in our union,
Ons gemeenskap maak ons sterk	Solidarity makes us surge.

Koor (x2)	*Refrain (x2)*
Skou'aan skouer in die suide	*Shoulder to shoulder in the South;*
Spel ons die toekoms uit	*The future let us face.*
Die Internasionale	*In the Internationale*
Mensdom staan gelyk	*We are all the human race.*

Geen bygelowe kan ons ophef	Unreason will not raise us,
Geen gerustheid kan ons baat	Nor complacency or fate
Slegs self kan ons die kettings afgooi	Chains we alone must break off
Van gierigheid en haat	And ban avarice and hate.
Ellende, honger kom tot einde	Hunger, misery will not stop us,
Die aardse diewe sal moet vort	Base thievery must end.
Soldate sal hul by die stakings	Soldiers: stand with us, the strikers,
Oorlog ewig opgeskort	Forever warfare we suspend.

Belgian/ Walloon Cercle littéraire wallon   ***French-related language in Southern Belgium***

Lèvez-ve tos les cis qui sos l'tére	Stand up, you wretched of the earth.
Ovrèt po n'nin t'esse èl mizère	And all those who suffer woe
Turtos essonle nos alans mostrer	All of us will now show you
Qui nos n'sèrans pu dominés	We won't bow to any foe.
Nos volans d'ner à nos-èfants	To our children we will give
Di l'ovrèdje, del djôye èt dè pan.	Labor, joy, and ample bread.

Nos nos batrans tot come nos péres
Zèls qui nos ont scrî nos'istwére.

Refrain (x2)
C'ést l'dièrin-ne bataye
Qui nos fans as canayes
Is-arant leû daye
Voleûrs èt profiteûs. (x2)

Fini dè profiter d'nos fwèces
Po nos ôtes, c'èst nosse seûle ritchesse
Nos n'volans pu passer po brubeûs
Ca nos-avans ossi dès dreûts
Fât qu'lès pouris rindèsse des comptes
Unis, nos mosteurans â monde
Qui l'pu fwèrt des pârtis sèrèt
Li grand parti dès cis qu'ovrét.

We will fight as did our kin,
Those who wrote our lives to read.

Refrain (x2)
It's the final conflict,
We're fighting for our lives
Against profiteers and thieves
And those who call us knaves.

They make profit from our health,
All our labor, all our wealth.
But we are no longer brutes,
We all demand our rights.
The corrupt must give what's owed.
United we will show the world.
For we are building hand in hand
The great party of the working man.

The Cercle littéraire wallon published poetry in Walloon from its founding in 1909 but was most active in the 1920s and 1930s.

Catalan

Amunt els damnats de la terra
Amunt els qui pateixen fam.
La força pel dret és vençuda,
S'acosta el bell temps de la pau.
Del passat destruïm misèries,
Esclaus aixequeu vostres cors,
La terra serà tota nostra,
No hem estat res i ho serem tot.

Refrany (x2)
És la lluita final,
unim-nos i demà
la internacional(
serà el gènere humà.

1930s Eastern Iberian Peninsula

Arise all those who suffer hunger,
All the wretched of the land.
Tyranny will be defeated,
The hour of peace is at hand.
All past misery we will destroy.
Break free, you slaves, no more in thrall.
The earth is ours to now enjoy.
We were naught; we will be all.

Refrain (x2)
Comrades come rally,
The last fight let us face.
The Internationale
Shall be the human race.

No esperes salvacions supremes
De déus, de reis ni de tirans,
Obrer, és la sang de tes venes
La que triomfant et salvarà.
La força del tirà sotmesat
On puny deixarà quan voldràs;
Atiem la fornal encesa,
El ferro és fill del nostre braç.

Expect no help from lofty saviors,
From tyrant, god, or any peer.
Workers, the blood that in you courses—
That will triumph over fear.
The tyrant's power provokes resistance.
You can beat it, yes you can.
We will ignite the fiery forge,
And shape the iron with our own hands.

Refrany

Refrain

Obrers, camperols, la batalla
Ha començat i finirà,
La terra és per qui la treballa,
Qui no treballe morirà.
Si del cel de la nostra terra
Foragitem dels corbs l'estol,
Pau ferma seguirà a la Guerra
Sempre més brillarà el sol.

Workers, farmers, join the fight.
Producers all, we earn our bread.
The world belongs by to us by right.
The idle rich's rule is dead.
From the core of our new world
We'll expel those birds of prey.
Peace will follow after war,
And the sun will shine all day.

Refrany

Refrain

Source: University of Valencia [a province with a significant Catalan-speaking population]
https://www.uv.es/~pla/red.net/intsong.hml

Dutch

Ontwaak, verworpen van der aarde
Ontwaak verdoemte in hongers sfeer
Reedlijk willen stroomt over de aarde
En de stroom rijst al meer tot meer
Sterft, je oude formen en gedachten
Slaafgeboornen, ontwaak, ontwaak
De wereld steut op niewe krachten
Begeerte heeft ons aangeraakt

Wake up, all you condemned to hunger,
All outcasts of the earth.
So strongly flows the voice of reason
From sea to sea and berth to berth.
Let outdated doctrine be abandoned
Wake up slaves, no more in thrall.
The world will rise on new foundations,
Desire for justice is our call.

Chorus (x2)
Makkers, ten laaste male
*Tot de strijd ons geschaardt**
En de Internationale
Zal morgen heerschen op aard

Refrain
Comrades, come rally
*And the battle let us fight.**
The Internationale
Will show the world the morning light.

De staat verdrukt, de wet is gelogen
De rijkaard leeft zelfzuchtig voort
Tot merg en been wordt de arme uitgezorgen
En zijn recht is een ijdel word
Wil zijn het moe naar andere wilt e leven
Broeders hoert hoe gelykheid spreekt
Geen recht, waar plicht is opgeheven
Geen plicht, leert zij, waar recht ontbreeekt.

The state oppresses, the law's a lie
The selfish rich live well.
Marrow to bone they suck us dry
Our rights an empty shell.
Brothers, sisters, hark to equality
The rulers' norms we will fight.
Away with rights that disdain all duty,
Away with duties without rights.

Chorus
De heerschers door duiwelste listen
Bedwelmen ons met bloedigen damp
Broeders, strijd niet meer voor andere twisten
Breek de rijen! Hier is u kamp.

Refrain
Devils' wiles deploy the rulers,
Drugging us with bloody damp.
Do not be lured in their disputes,
Break the reins and join our camp.

Gij die ons tot helden wilt maken
O, barbaren, denkt wat ge doet.
Wij haven waap'nen hem te raaken
Die dorstige schijnen naar ons bloed.

To you who want to make us heroes,
To our enemies, think and break!
We have weapons, we will strike
And put your bloodlust on the stake!

*The version from the Flemish-speaking parts of Belgium has a slightly different refrain:

*Makkers, hort de signal**
Tot de strijd ons geschaardt
En de Internationale
Zal morgen heerschen op aard

Galician   *Iberian Language: Northwest Spain*

En pé, escravos da terra	Stand up, all enslaved on earth
En pé, os que non teñem pan	Arise, all those who have no bread
A nosa razón forte berra	Our reason rumbles in our bellows
O triunfo chega en volcán	Exploding triumph up ahead,
Crebemos o xugo do pasado	The yoke of history we will shatter.
Pobo de servos, ergue xa	Break free you slaves, no more in thrall,
Que o mundo vai ser transformado	The world will rise on new foundations,
E unha orde nova va reinar	And its realm will hold us all.

Axuntémonos todas	*Comrades, come rally*
E a loita final.	*And the last fight let us face.*
O xénero humano	*The Internationale*
Forma a internacional	*Unites the human race.*
Axuntémonos todos	
E a loita final	
O xénero humano	
Forma a internacional	

No hay salvadores supremos	Expect no help from lofty saviors.
Nin rei, nin tribune, nin deus	No faith have we in prince, god, or boss.
Tenemos que salvarnos nós mesmos	We ourselves must now muster
O pobo travallador	The strength to save the working class.
Para que nos devolvan o roubador	To make the robbers return our goods,
Para derrubar esta prisión	To abolish our debtor's lot,
Batamos no lume sagrado	Let us heat the sacred forge,
Ferreiros dun mundo mellor	Strike the iron when it is hot.

[Galician refrain summons first all women—*todas*—then all men—*todos*]

German (SPD, 1890s; KPD 1919)   (Emil Luckhardt; 1896)

Wacht auf, Verdammte dieser Erde,	Wake up, all condemned to hunger.
die stets man noch zum Hungern zwingt!	You wretched of the earth.
Das Recht wie Glut im Kraterherde	For justice blasts from its crater

nun mit Macht zum Durchbruch dringt.
Reinen Tisch macht mit dem Bedränger!
Heer der Sklaven, wache auf!
Ein Nichts zu sein, tragt es nicht länger
Alles zu werden, strömt zuhauf!

Now our power will end the dearth.
Wipe the slate of our oppressor,
Wake up slaves, no more in thrall.
We have been naught, but no longer,
From now on, we will be all.

Chor (x2)
Völker, hört die Signale!
Auf zum letzten Gefecht!
Die Internationale
erkämpft das Menschenrecht.

Refrain (x2)
People, listen to the message,
Ready for the final fight
The Internationale
Leads the battles for human rights.

Es rettet uns kein höh'res Wesen,
kein Gott, kein Kaiser noch Tribun
Uns aus dem Elend zu erlösen
können wir nur selber tun!
Leeres Wort: des Armen Rechte,
Leeres Wort: des Reichen Pflicht!
Unmündig nennt man uns und Knechte,
duldet die Schmach nun länger nicht!

No higher being there is can save us:
No god, no ruler, or tribune.
They want no more than to enslave us
We must free ourselves alone.
Empty words: the rights of paupers.
Or the duties of the rich.
To them we're merely hands or servants.
All these insults we will ditch.

In Stadt und Land, ihr Arbeitsleute,
Wir sind die stärkste der Partei'n
Die Müßiggänger schiebt beiseite!
Diese Welt muss unser sein;
Unser Blut sei nicht mehr der Raben,
Nicht der mächt'gen Geier Fraß!
Erst wenn wir sie vertrieben haben
dann scheint die Sonn' ohn' Unterlass!

In town and field, come on all toilers,
Join our party and all who work.
The world belongs to those who change it.
No more room here for the shirk.
Our blood will not feed the vultures;
We're not their fodder or their prey.
Only when we banish them forever
Then the sun will shine all day.

German II: (Erich Weinert, 1929)

GDR: East Germany: 1971

Auf, ihr Verdammte des Planeten
Auf, Hungerknechte, aus dem Sumpf
Vernunft bricht aus dem Morgenröten,

Stand up, all enslaved to hunger
All oppressed on planet earth.
Reason rumbles with the thunder

Aus Schlündern donnert sie Triumph.
Macht endlich Schluß mit dem Gewesnen!
Es stürtzt die Welt. Der Tag ist nah.
Denn heut sind wir die Auserlesnen.
Wir waren nichts, jetzt sind wir da!

And at dawn a new world's in birth.
Clear the slate of old traditions,
The world up-turned, the day is nigh.
From today we are the chosen.
We were naught, now rising high.

Chor
Zum letzten Kampf! Ihr alle,
Ihr Völker im Verein
Die Internationale
Wird alle Menschen sein

Refrain
Comrades come rally,
The last fight let us face!
The Internationale
Unites the human race.

Wir wissen, daß uns glücklich mache
Kein Gott, kein Kaiser, kein Tribün.
Genossen, unsrer Freiheit Sache
Kann nur in unsren Händen ruhn!
Packt, bis es brüllt, das Ungeheuer,
Und schafft dem Geist ein freies Gleis!
Wir blasen jetzt in eigne Feuer.
Schlagt auf den Stahl, er ist noch heiß!

We know what changes will delight us:
No God, no ruler, no tribune.
Comrades, it's our cause to fight thus,
We must free ourselves alone.
Squeeze the menace until defeat,
And for our goals clear an open plot.
We must raise the forge's heat,
And strike now while the iron is hot.

Chor

Refrain

Staat und Gesetz geht über Leichen.
Die Steuer wird zum Massenmord.
Wo gibt es Pflichten für den Reichen?
Des Armen Recht, ein leeres Wort!

State and law have crushed our corpses.
Taxes weigh us down to death.
Empty words, the rights of paupers,
Likewise, the duties of the rich.

Genug! Es sprechen jetzt die Knechte,
Und das Gesetz der Gleichheit spricht:
Nicht eine Pflicht mehr ohne Rechte
Und keine Rechte ohne Pflicht!

Enough! Now underdogs speak up.
Equality we will now enforce.
No more rights without duties.
No more duties without rights endorsed.

Abscheulich blähn sich diese Götzen,
Die Herren von Schacht und Eisenbahn
Sie haben unser Blut tu Schätzen,

Fat and bloated they sit like idols,
Masters of the rail and mine.
They have drained our blood and vitals.

Sie haben unser Gut vertan.	The rich waste what's ours, and all confine
In Stahlresoren liegt's vergraben.	In iron coffers buried deep.
Wann machen wir die Rechnung glatt?	It's time to even up the stakes!
Das Volk will ja nur wiederhaben,	The people want what's ours to keep.
Was man dem Volk gestohlen hat.	Our stolen goods they must forsake.

Die Herrscher machten uns betrunken.	The rulers drug us with their lies.
Der Zauber muß zu Ende sein.	Their hocus-pocus must end now.
Drum werft ins Heer der Freiheit Funken!	Stun their army with freedom's light
Drum schlägt es mit dem Kolben drein.	And hit them harder on the brow.
Wenn sie uns zwingen, die Barbaren,	And if they still try to draft us,
Soldat zu spielen noch einmal,	To serve as soldiers one more time,
Wir werden unsre Kugeln sparen	We will hold our ammunition,
Für unsren eignen General.	And turn our fire on generals' crimes.

Arbeiter, Bauern, kommt zum Ende!	Workers, farmers join the fight.
Wir sind der Schaffenden Partei!	The producers' party we defend.
Die Welt gehört in unsre Hände.	The world belongs to us by right,
Der Reichen Schonzeit ist vorbei.	The rich men's privilege at an end.
Sie sogen Blut aus unsren Wunden	Strip them of their phony culture,
Reißt ihnen ab den Heiligenschein!	From our wounds our blood they drain.
Erst wenn das Geiervolk verschwunden	Only when we chase off vultures,
Wird unsre Welt voll Sonne sein	Can our world have light again.

Die Internationale von Eugène Pottier, German Translation, Erich Weinert. Woodcuts: Frans Masreel (Berlin [East]: Rütten & Loenig, 1971). This centennial edition reprinted Weinert's version which was sung in the GDR: 1948–1989.

Italian (Partito Socialista Italiano, 1921)   **Italian Socialist Party**

Compagni avanti, il gran Partito	Comrades, forward with our party,
Noi siamo dei lavoratori.	Workers, toilers, all are we.
Rosso un fiore in petto c'è fiorito	On our chests a red rose blossoms,
Una fede ci è nata in cuor.	As does our faith in solidarity.
Noi non siamo più nell'officina,	We are no longer locked in labor,

Entro terra, dai campi, al mar	In office, pasture, or at sea.
La plebe sempre all'opra china	Against the odds the people struggle,
Senza ideale in cui sperar.	Without ideals we will be free.

Coro (x2)
Su, lottiamo! l'ideale
Nostro alfine sarà
L'Internazionale
Futura umanità!

Refrain (x2)
Come and join the struggle
The last fight let us face
The Internationale
Unites the human race.

Un gran stendardo al sol fiammante	See our banner flaming red,
Dinanzi a noi glorioso va,	Lighting up our glorious way.
Noi vogliam' per esso giù infrante	We aspire to break and shed
Le catene alla libertà!	The chains that limit freedom's sway.
Che giustizia venga noi chiediamo:	No more bosses, no more servants,
Non più servi, non più signor;	May justice give us guiding light.
Fratelli tutti esser vogliamo	Brothers, sisters, our wish is fervent:
Nella famiglia del lavor.	Solidarity our cause to fight.

Coro

Refrain

Lottiam', lottiam', la terra sia	Come fight for world and our neighbors,
Di tutti eguale proprietà,	And for equal ownership.
Più nessuno nei campi dia	No longer will we who labor
L'opra ad altri che in ozio sta.	Yield our goods to idle rich.

E la macchina sia alleata	And the machines will be our allies,
Non nemica ai lavorator;	Supporting those like us who sweat.
Così la vita rinnovata	In transforming all our lives
All'uom darà pace ed amor!	Our cause brings peace and love and bread.

Avanti, avanti, la vittoria	Onward, on to victory,
è nostra e nostro è l'avvenir;	And the future will be ours.
Più civile e giusta, la storia	A world we seek more just and fairer,
Un'altra era sta per aprir.	A whole new era is in flower.
Largo a noi, all'alta battaglia	Let us march into the battle.

Noi corriamo per l'Ideal:

Via, largo, noi siam la canaglia

Che lotta pel suo Germinal!

We desire an ideal earth.

Even if they call us scoundrels,

We will win this world in birth.

Coro

Refrain

Adaptation attributed to Ettore Marroni (1875–1943)

Brazilian Portuguese (1930s)

De pé, ó vitimas da fome

De pé, famélicos da terra

Da ideia a chama já consome

A crosta bruta que a soterra

Cortai o mal bem pelo fundo

De pé, de pé, não mais senhores

Se nada somos em tal mundo

Sejamos tudo, ó produtores.

Arise all condemned to hunger

The pariahs of the earth

Our ideal erupts like thunder

From below, a new world's in birth

Pull up the old that has bound us,

Stand up, resist the boss's call.

In this world we have been no-one,

We workers shall now be all.

Refrão

Bem unidos façamos

Nesta luta final

Uma terra sem amos

A Internacional

Refrain

This final conflict

United we shall now face

In a land without bosses

The Internationale claims our place

Senhores, Patrões, chefes supremos*

Nada esperamos de nenhum

Sejamos nós que conquistemos

A terra mãe livre e comum

Para não ter protestos vãos

Para sair desse antro estreito

Façamos nós por nossas mãos

Tudo o que a nós nos diz respeito.

From gentlemen, and all big bosses

We want nothing more at all.

It will now be us who go on to conquer

This land in common for us all.

We will launch no vacant protests.

We will quit this narrow cave.

We will confront them with our hands.

Respect for us they can no longer waive.

O crime do rico a lei o cobre

The state crushes and oppresses us.

O Estado esmaga o oprimido
Não há direitos para o pobre
Ao rico tudo é permitido
À opressão não mais sujeitos
Somos iguais todos os seres
Não mais deveres sem direit
Não mais direitos sem deveres.

But protects the rich by law.
The elite does as it pleases
But the poor's rights are naught.
Now oppression cannot subdue us.
We want equal human rights
No more rights without duties!
No more duties shorn of rights!

Abomináveis na grandeza
Os reis da mina e da fornalha
Edificaram a riqueza
Sobre o suor de quem trabalha
Todo o produto de quem sua
A corja rica o recolheu
Querendo que ela o restitua
O povo só quer o que é seu.

Despise them for their grandee airs:
Kings of industry and soil.
It's time to teach them and their peers
About our sweat and all our toil.
Our labor's yield is locked away
In the coffers of a few.
In demanding their restitution
The people only ask their due.

Refrão

Refrain

Nós fomos de fumo embriagados
Paz entre nós, guerra aos senhores
Façamos greve de soldados
Somos irmãos, trabalhadores
Se a raça vil, cheia de galas
Nos quer à força canibais
Logo verás que as nossas balas
São para os nossos generais.

From drunken stupors we have risen
The bosses we will fight.
Soldiers will come and join us
In solidarity we have might.
As a multitude we are stronger
Than their cannibalistic blight.
We will soon turn our weapons
On all generals we have in sight.

Pois somos do povo os ativos
Trabalhador forte e fecundo
Pertence a Terra aos produtivos
Ó parasitas deixai o mundo
Ó parasitas que te nutres
Do nosso sangue a gotejar
Se nos faltarem os abutres
Não deixa o sol de fu\lgurar!

We the people are more active,
Working, toilng, we are strong.
The world belong to us, producers,
Not to parasites, who are wrong.
How many on our blood have feasted?
Those rapacious birds of prey!
We will dispense with all those vultures.
When they go, the sun will stay.

Peninsula (Iberian) Portuguese

*Differs from the Brazilian in verse 2, line 1:
Messias, Deus, chefes supremos
[From] Messiah, God, and all big bosses

Portuguese Socialist Party, which emerged after the death of dictator António de Oliveira Salazar in 1970

Russian (Arkady Yakovievich Kots)	Published: *Listki Zhizni*, (London, 1902)

Vstavaj prokliatem zaklejmennyj,	Arise, those damned to bondage
Ves mir golodnykh i rabov!	The starving of the world
Kipit nash razum vozmushchionnyj	Our conscience is boiling up for action,
I v smertnyj boj vesti gotov.	To the battle unto death.
Ves mir nasilia my razrushim	Down to its foundation
Do osnovania, a zatem	Will we strip this coercive state.
My nash my novyj mir postroim,	We will build the new world up from nothing
Kto byl nikem tot stanet vsem!	We have been naught; we will be all.
Pripev:	*Refrain*
Ehto est nash poslednij	*Stand up and rally*
I reshitelnyj boj	*For the decisive fight!!*
S Internatsionalom	*The Internationale*
Vosprianet rod liudskoj	*Shall be our guiding light!!*
Nikto ne dast nam izbavlenia:	No one on high will deliver us.
Ni bog, ni tsar i ne geroj	No god, no hero or the tsar.
Dobiomsia my osvobozhdenia	We will achieve our liberation
Svoeiu sobstvennoj rukoj.	By our own collective hand.
Chtob svergnut gniot rukoj umeloj,	With our hands we'll crush oppression,
Otvoevat svoio dobro,	We'll reclaim what's ours by right.
Vzduvajte gorn i kujte smelo,	Take the hammer and forge now boldly,

Poka zhelezo goriacho!   Striking while the iron is hot.
A darmoedov vsekh doloj!

Lish my, rabotniki vsemirnoj   Only great labor's army
Velikoj armii truda!   Spread across the earth,
Vladet zemlioj imeem pravo,   Only we and not the parasites,
No parazity - nikogda!   Have the right to rule the earth.

I esli grom velikij grianet   And if a thunder-storm comes down
Nad svoroj psov i palachej,   On executioners and dogs,
Dlia nas vsio takzhe solntse stanet   The sun will still beam down on us,
Siiat ogniom svoikh luchej.   Our bright new day will dawn.

Arkady Yakovievich Kots (1872–1943) studied metallurgy in France, where he heard the *Internationale* in 1899. This translation appeared in *Listki Zhizn* [Leaflets from Life, 1902] published in London under the pen-name A. Danin.

Source:
www.marxists.org

Russian version in Cyrillic script follows on the next page

Интернационал
Вставай проклятьем заклейменный,
Весь мир голодных и рабов!
Кипит наш разум возмущённый
И в смертный бой вести готов.
Весь мир насилья мы разрушим
До основанья, а затем
Мы наш мы новый мир построим,
Кто был никем тот станет всем!

Припев:
Это есть наш последний
И решительный бой
С Интернационалом
Воспрянет род людской

Никто не даст нам избавленья:
Ни бог, ни царь и не герой
Добьёмся мы освобожденья
Своею собственной рукой.
Чтоб свергнуть гнёт рукой умелой,
Отвоевать своё добро,
Вздувайте горн и куйте смело,
Пока железо горячо!

Лишь мы, работники всемирной
Великой армии труда!
Владеть землёй имеем право,
Но паразиты - никогда!
И если гром великий грянет
Над сворой псов и палачей,
Для нас всё также солнце станет
Сиять огнём своих лучей.

Spanish; Castilian (Socialist)

(2nd Spanish Republic: 1931–39)

¡Arriba parias de la tierra!
¡En pie famélica legion!
Atruena la razón en marcha
Es el fin de la opresión.
Del pasado hay que hacer añicos
¡Legión esclava en pie vencer!
El mundo va a cambiar de base
Los nada de hoy todo han der ser.

Arise all you condemned to hunger!
You pariahs of the earth!
Reason rising with the thunder
Oppression's dead, a world's in birth.
Historic bonds we must now shatter
Slaves, stand up and heed the call!
The world is changing for the better
We have been naught, will now be all

Estribillo (x2)
Agrupémos todos
En la luche final
El género humano
Es la internacional

Refrain
Comrades come rally
And the last fight let us face.
The Internationale
Unites the human race.

Ni en dioses, reyes, ni tribunos
Está el supremo Salvador
Nosotros mismos realicemos
El esfuerzo redentor.
Para hacer que el tirano caiga
Y el mundo esclavo liberar
Soplemos la potente fragua
Que el hombre libre ha de forjar

Expect no help from lofty saviors.
No faith have we in prince or peer.
We ourselves must now muster
The fortitude to dispel fear.
To make the hated tyrant fall,
And ensure all slaves go free
We must ignite the fiery forge
For which free people hold the key.

Estribillo (x2)

Refrain (x2)

La ley nos burla y el Estado
Oprime y sangra al productor
Nos da derechos irrisorios
No hay deberes el señor.
Basta ya de tutela odiosa
Que la igualdad ha de ser
No más deberes sin derechos
Ningún derecho sin deber.

The law will cheat us, as will the state.
Their taxes make us bleed.
Our so-called rights have little weight,
The rich their duties do not heed.
We've had enough of condescension.
New laws we need for equal light.
Away with rights that know no duty.
Away with duties shorn of rights.

Estribillo (x2)

Refrain (x2)

Source: University of Valencia, Spain
https://www.uv.es/~pla/red.net/intsong.html

Castilian II: Federación Anarquista Ibérica   Iberian Anarchist Federation (est. 1927)

¡Arriba los pobres del mundo!

¡En pie los esclavos sin pan.

Alcémonos todos que llega

La Revolución Social.

La Anarquía ha de emanciparnos

De toda la explotación.

El comunismo libertario

Será nuestra redención

Estribillo (x2)

Agrupémonos todos

A la lucha final

Con la FAI lograrmos

El éxito final

Color de sangre tiene el fuego

Color negro tiene el volcán

Colores rojo y negro tiene

Nuestra bandera triunfal.

Los hombres han de ser hermanos

Cese la desigualdad.

La Tierra será paraíso

Libre de la humanidad

Estribillo (x2)

Stand up, all oppressed by hunger

Poor people of the world!

To make our social revolution

Let us unite to work.

From all sorts of exploitation

Anarchism will make us free.

Radical communalism

Will bring about our destiny.

Refrain

Comrades, come rally.

The last fight let us face.

With the anarchist federation

We'll win the human race.

Our blood like fire is deepest red.

Like volcanic lava, the color black

Joins with fire to weave the thread

To make the flag that will fight back.

We fight to end inequality.

Solidarity must be our goal.

Seek a utopian polity

That will make all humans whole.

Refrain (x2)

Spanish: Latin American   **Chile, Cuba, Peru, and Uruguay**

¡Arriba los pobres del mundo!   Stand up, all enslaved by hunger
de pie los esclavos sin pan   Stand up, poor people of the earth
y gritemos todos unidos   And let us shout to one another
viva la internacional!   Hail the *Internationale*'s birth.
removamos todas las ramas   Let us shake off all the chains
que nos impiden nuestro bien*   That impede our goal for good.*
cambiemos al mundo de base   Change our world from its foundation.
un viento al imperio burgués   Blow away bourgeois dead wood.

Estribillo   *Refrain*
agrupémonos todos   *Comrades, come rally*
en la lucha final   *And may the people rise*
y se alzen los pueblos   *The Internationale*
por la internacional   *Is our collective prize*
agrupémonos todos   *Comrades, come rally*
en la lucha final   *And still bolder they will rise*
y se alzen los pueblos con valor   *The Internationale*
por la Internacional   *Is our collective prize*

el dia que el triunfo alcancemos   The day of triumph we will achieve
ni esclavos ni hambrientos habrá   No more starvelings or slaves
la tierra sera el paraiso   The earth and all will be an Eden,
de toda la humanidad   Humanity new and brave.

que la tierra de todos sus frutos   Let the land yield all its harvest,
y la dicha en nuestro hogar   And let it thus enhance our health.
El trabajo será el sostén que todos   Work will sustain us all the farthest.
De la abundancia gozar   Enjoy abundance and our wealth.

Estribillo   *Refrain*

Altenative line 6 in Colombia:
(also sung in Cuba):
Que oprimen al proletario/   That oppress the proletariat

(https://www.ecured.cu/La_Internacional)

Estatales CLATA: Confederación Latinoamericana y del Caribe de las Trabajadoras y Trabajadores (Also in Cuba: this medley, a samba version, comes after the standard marching version.) https://www.youtube.com/watch?v=-FRmSwhjM3g

And by Quilapayún, Chilean group singing since the 1960s:
https://www.letras.com/quilapayun/946135/

Spanish: Colombian	**Associated with the 1980s guerrilla movement.**
¡Arriba los pobres del mundo!	Stand up, all enslaved by hunger.
De pie los esclavos sin pan	Stand up, poor people of the earth.
y gritemos todos Unidos	And let's proclaim to one another
viva la internacional!	The *Internationale*'s birth.
Removamos todas las trabas	All chains that bind the proletariat
que oprimen al proletario	Let us destroy for good,
cambiemos al mundo de base	Change our world from its foundation,
un viento al imperio burgués	Sweep away bourgeois dead wood.

Estribillo	*Refrain*
agrupémonos todos	*Comrades, come rally*
en la lucha final	*And may the people rise.*
y se alzen los pueblo	*The Internationale*
por la internacional	*Is our collective prize*
agrupémonos todos	*Comrades, come rally*
en la lucha final	*And still bolder they will rise*
y se alzen los pueblos con valor	*The Internationale*
por la Internacional	*Is our collective prize*

No más salvadors supremos	Expect no more from saviors,
Ni césar, ni burgués, ni dios	Caesar, bourgeois, any god.
Que nosotros mismos haremos	We alone will save us.
Nuestra propia redención.	Our own road we will have trod.

Los que quieren los proletarios	We proletarians are now seeking
El disfrute de su bien	To enjoy all that we've gained.
Tenemos que ser los obreros	As workers we should be leading
Los que guiemos el trén.	And we should now drive the train.

Estribillo
El dia que el triunfo alcancemos
Ni esclavos ni dueños habrá.
Los odios que al mundo envenan
Al mundo se extinguirán
El hombre del hombre es hermano
Cese la desigualdad
La tierra será el Paraiso
Bello de la humanidad.

Refrain
The day of triumph let us strive for
No more masters, no more slaves.
The hate with which they drug us,
All their violence sweep away.
Together we are brothers,
Inequality must go.
The earth and all will be an Eden
Where humanity will grow.

Estribillo

Refrain

Sung by Los Escamilla, associated with the 19th of April guerrilla group in Colombia

Spanish: Argentine

¡De pie, malditos de la Tierra!
¡Alzad, esclavos del dolor!
El genio truena en la montaña,
Y en su antorcha, la erupción.
El pasado todo arrasemos,
¡Turba esclava, de pie, de pie!
El mundo cambiara de bases,
Hoy nada sois, todo seréis.

Arise all enslaved by want
You wretched of the earth,
A new spirit thunders in the mountains
And a better world's in birth.
Wipe the slate of past traditions,
The oppressed to arms we now will call.
The earth will rise on new foundations.
We have been naught; we shall be all.

Estribillo (x2)
En la lucha postrera,
Nuestra unión triunfará.
La Internacional
Será la humanidad.

Refrain
In the ultimate conflict,
Let all stand in place.
The international
Shall be the human race.

Spanish: Mexican

¡Arriba los pobres del mundo!
¡Arriba, todos a luchar
por la justicia proletaria!
Un nuevo mundo nace ya
  Destrocemos todas las cadenas
de esclavitud tradicional,
y quienes nunca fueron nada
dueños del mundo hoy serán

Stand up, all those who struggle,
Poor people of the earth
For revolutionary justice.
A better world's in birth.
Ancient bondage and tradition,
Let us destroy their thrall
And we who have been nothing,
We will soon be all.

Estribillo
A la lucha, proletarios,
al combate final,
y se alcen los pueblos
por la Internacional

Refrain
Comrades, come rally,
And may the people rise
The Internationale
Is our collective prize.

A la lucha, proletarios,
al combate final,
y se alcen los pueblos con valor
por la Internacional

Comrades, come rally
And still bolder we will rise.
The Internationale
Is our collective prize.

Ya no queremos salvadores
que sirvan sólo al capital,
en adelante los obreros
impondrán su voluntad
Al burgués quitemos lo robado
y todos juntos, libres ya,
por el deber decidiremos
y cada quien lo cumplirá

Against those who claim to save us
But who fit the bosses' bill,
All you workers to the vanguard!
We will impose our will.
Bourgeois thieves must yield their booty.
All together act as one;
It's for us to decide our duty,
And for all to pay their dues.

Estribillo

Refrain

Nosotros los trabajadores
del mundo, ejercito de paz,
debemos poseer la tierra

Workers of the world unite
As ambassadors for peace
For those who work, a shining light

que nos roba el holgazán
Y el gran trueno rasgue las tinieblas
que cierran paso a la verdad,
y cuando nuestra aurora surja
un nuevo mundo alumbrará

Estribillo

For all shirking must cease.
Revolutionary lighting strips the darkness
And will lead the way to truth
And our bright morning surges
A new world's in birth.

Refrain

Yiddish: das internatsyonale Zinglid

Shtayt oyf ir ale, ver vi shlafn
In hinger leybn miz, in noit
Der gayst, er kokht, er rift tzi wafn
In shlakht indz firn iz er greyt
Di velt fin gwaldtatn in leydn
Tseshtern weln mir in dan
In frayheyt, glaykhh a Gan-Ayden
Beshafn vet der arbetsman.

Tsuzung (x2)
Dus vet zayn shoyn der letster
In antshaydener shtrayt
Mit dem internatsyonal
Shtayt oyf, ir arbetsleyt

Nayn, kayner vet indz nisht befrayen
Nisht Got alayn in nisht kayn held
Mir indzer eygenem klei-zayin
Derleyzung brengen mir der welt
Arup dem yokh! Genig gelitn
Genig fargosn blit in shvays.
Tsebluzt dus fayer, lomir shmidn
Kolzman dus ayzn iz nokh heys

Tsuzung

The International Anthem

Stand up all of you in bondage,
Enduring hunger, deepest plight
The spirit boils and calls to weapons,
To battle, ready for a fight.
We workers will destroy then—
The world of violence, full of grief.
Our freedom will be an Eden-garden,
Where we workers find relief.

Refrain (x2)
Stand up and rally
For this decisive fight.
The Internationale
Is the workers' light.

No-one else will come to free us,
No kaiser, hero, and no god.
With weapons now in our own hands,
We will redeem the world.
Enough of suffering and sweat.
Stand up now and drop the yoke.
The fire and the forge are ours now.
Let's strike while the iron is hot.

Refrain

Der arbetsman vet zayn memshala
Farshpraytn oyf der gantser erd
Di parazitn di mapule
Bakimen veln fin zayn shvert
Di groyse shturemteg zay veln
Nor far tiranen shreklekh zayn
Zay konen ober nisht farsteln
Far indz die hele zinen shayn.

   Tsuzung.

We workers and our dominion
Spread across the entire earth,
From our swords all parasites
Will feel our burning wrath.
The great storm is coming,
Which tyrants will confine.
They can no longer block our way.
Our bright new light will shine.

   Refrain

The Yiddish script follows on the next page.

די אינטערנאציאנאלע זינגליד

שטייט אויף, איר אלע, װער װי שקלאפֿן,
אין הונגער לעבן מוח, אין נויט!
דער גײסט - ער קאָכט, ער רופֿט צו װאָפֿן
אין שלאַכט אונדז פֿירן איז ער גרייט.
די װעלט פֿון גװאַלדטאַטן און לײדן
צעשטערן װעלן מיר און דאַן
פֿון פֿרײהײט, גלײכהײט אַ גן־עֶדֶן
באַשאַפֿן װעט דער אַרבעטסמאַן.

[צחזון:] [x2]

דאָס װעט זײַן שוין דער לעצטער
און ענטשידענער שטרײַט!
מיט דעם אינטערנאצִיאָנאל
שטייט אויף, איר אַרבעטסלײַט!

נײַן, קײנער װעט אונדז ניט באַפֿרײַען:
ניט גאָט אלײן און ניט קײן העלד־
מיט אונדער אייגענעם כֹּל־זײַן
דערלײזונג ברענגען מיר דער װעלט.
אַראָפ דעם יאָך! גענוג געליטן,
גענוג פֿאַרגאָסן בלוט און שװייס!
צעבלאָזט דעם פֿײַער, לאָמיר שמידן
כֹּל־זמאַן דאָס אײַזן איז נאָך הייס!

דער אַרבעטסמאַן װעט זײַן מֶמשָׁלָה
פֿערשפרייטן אויף דער גאַנצער ערד,
און פֿאַראיזטן די מַפָּלָה
באַקומען װעלן פֿון זײַן שװערד.
די גרויסע שטורעם־טעג זיי װעלן
נאָר פֿאַר טיראַנען שרעקלעכער זײַן;
זיי קאָנען אָבער ניט פֿאַרשטעלן
פֿון אונדז די העלע זונען־שײַן.

Zulu: i-Internationale	**South African Communist Party**
N'zigqila zezwe lonke	Arise all enslaved, oppressed!
Vukan'ejokwen'lobugqili	Wake up, shake off your chains.
Sizokwakh'umhlaba kabusha	We will make a brand new world,
Siqed'indlala nobumpofu.	And end starvation for the poor.
Lamasik'okusibopha	Let us cut the bonds that hold us.
Asilwise yonk'incindezelo	We have suffered every woe.
Manj'umhlab'unesakhiw'esisha	Now a new world is ripening.
Asisodwa Kulomkhankaso.	We alone can make it grow.
Maqaban'wozan'sihlanganeni	*Let us rise and take the path,*
Sibhekene nempi yamanqamu	*The final battle we await.*
I-Internationale	*The Internationale*
Ibumb'uluntu lonke.	*Will shape all human clay.*

Sung by exiles in South African Communist Party (SACP) in the Soviet Union and elsewhere in Europe and Africa (1950–90). Revived in country by returning exiles in the 1990s.

Eugène Pottier's Grave in Père Lachaise Cemetery.
Photographer unknown.
Courtesy of the Bibliothèque Nationale, Paris

SOURCES AND THANKS

Images: apart from the caricature on the cover, which comes from the Museum of the Hôtel de Ville, all images are reprinted as a courtesy to non-profit publication from the Bibliothèque Nationale of France.

Cover: Eugène Pottier. Caricature by Hippolyte Mailly. Published in *La Commune* 1871. Courtesy, Museum of the Hôtel de Ville, Paris.

Frontispiece: Eugène Pottier, songwriter. Photograph by Félix Tournachon, known as Nadar. Courtesy of the Bibliothèque Nationale de France.

Back cover: The Last Day of the Commune: Grand Panorama. Poster by Charles Castellani. Courtesy of the Bibliothèque Nationale, Paris.

Other images:

Napoleon Bonaparte Statue Toppled by Communards at the Place Vendome. April 1871. Photograph by Bruno Braquehais. Courtesy of the Bibliothèque Nationale, Paris.

Facsimile of Pierre Degeyter's score for the Internationale. *1888.* Courtesy of the Bibliothèque Nationale, Paris.

Communards Killed During Bloody Week, May 1871. Photograph by Eugène Disdéri. Courtesy of the Bibliothèque Nationale, Paris.

Eugène Pottier's Grave in Père Lachaise Cemetery. Photographer unknown. Courtesy of the Bibliothèque Nationale, Paris.

My thanks for assistance in Paris go to the librarians and image reproduction services of the Bibliothèque Nationale of France, to Sébastien Greppo and staff at the University of Chicago Paris Center, and to University of Chicago colleagues Robert Kendrick and Alison James for conversation about the Commune in word and music. In Chicago, thanks are due to the publishing team at Charles H. Kerr: Tamara L. Smith for editing and coordinating, Justin O'Brien for design, and Jim Marcus for the cover concept. In addition, thanks to Warren Leming for prompting me to send the proposal to this publisher; to Marc Silberman for encouraging the project; to Na'ama Rokem and Hoda El-Shakry for thoughts on the *Internationale* beyond Europe, and to David Graver for singing the *Internationale* and for much more.

INDEX OF POEMS AND SONGS

Books for a Better World

WALLS & BARS: Prisons & Prison Life in the "Land of the Free" by Eugene V. Debs; Introduction by David Dellinger. Both memoir & critique, this is one of the most insightful books ever written on prisons, by one of the most influential & best-loved radicals in U.S. history. *Revolutionary Classics.* 264 pages. $16.00

THE PULLMAN STRIKE, 130th Anniversary Edition, by Rev. William H. Carwardine with a new introduction by Peter Cole. Also includes the long out-of-print 1973 introduction and bibliography by Virgil J. Vogel. An eyewitness exposé and classic of labor journalism, industrial history, and strike-support activism. 216 pages. $18.00

COLD CHICAGO: A Haymarket Fable by Warren Leming, with illustrations by Carlos Cortez. A play in cabaret form with original music. *"Warren Leming's play on the Haymarket affair is the best antidote we have for the National Alzheimer's —our forgetfulness of yesterday"*—Studs Terkel. 112 pages. $15.00

VIVA POSADA! Edited and introduced by Carlos Cortez. Features 121 works by the popular engraver who inspired the Mexican muralists, the international Surrealist movement, and radical cartoonists all over the world. Includes classic texts on the artist by Jose Clemente Orozco, Frida Kahlo, André Breton, and others, plus more contemporary statements by Dennis Brutus, Rikki Ducornet, Lawrence Ferlinghetti, Robin D. G. Kelley, Franklin Rosemont, Joseph Jablonski, Ted Joans, and more. 96 pages. $13.00

WE WILL RETURN IN THE WHIRLWIND: Black Radical Organizing, 1960–1975, by Muhammad Ahmad, national field chairman of the Revolutionary Action Movement and founder of the African People's Party. Introduction by John Bracey. 340 pages. $18.00

JUICE IS STRANGER THAN FRICTION: Selected Writings of T-Bone Slim, edited & introduced by Franklin Rosemont. The IWW's greatest "Man of Letters" was an outstanding humorist, a wordplay genius, a presurrealist. *"T-Bone Slim has a lot to tell us, and does it well"*—Noam Chomsky. 160 pages. $10.00

ACCEPTABLE MEN: Life in the Largest Steel Mill in the World, a Memoir, by Noel Ignatiev. A firsthand account of everyday white supremacy, patriarchy, and the exploitation of labor, but also on-the-job resistance. 110 pages. $12.00

PRAISE BOSS! The Erotic Adventures of Mr. Block, a play by Joseph Grim Feinberg. The subject of Joe Hill's eponymous song and Ernest Riebe's cartoons, Mr. Block is the working class's biggest blockhead. 105 pages. $10.00

C H A R L E S H. K E R R
Est. 1886 / 8901 South Exchange Avenue, Chicago, Illinois 60617

A few words about the
CHARLES H. KERR
Publishing Company

"The Charles H. Kerr Company is a truly extraordinary example of living history. Here is the publisher of Gene Debs, Clarence Darrow, Mother Jones, Mary Marcy, Jack London, Carl Sandburg, and hundreds of other outstanding figures—still at it. Still fighting the good fight after a hundred glorious years. The American labor movement has a great heritage, and the Charles H. Kerr Company is a precious part of it. It deserves every support."—**Studs Terkel**

"What a remarkable history! How can it ever be estimated, the influence of the Kerr Company over all these years? Above all in this era of communication and the rising of the people all over the world, such a bond with expressions and education of the people must be truly celebrated—more than a statue of liberty: the Kerr Company is a true beacon."—**Meridel Le Sueur**

"Charles H. Kerr has a magnificent record. . . . More importantly, it continues that tradition of courageous publishing in these difficult times. Kerr's list of titles provides us with excellent material to continue the fight for a just society."—**Dennis Brutus**

The son of militant abolitionists, Charles Hope Kerr was a libertarian socialist, antiwar agitator, author, translator, vegetarian, and scholar. The publishing firm he founded in Chicago in 1886, a few weeks before Haymarket, is today the oldest alternative publishing house in the world. Many books recognized as classics in the fields of labor, socialism, feminism, history, anthropology, economics, civil liberties, animal rights, and radical ecology originally appeared under the Charles H. Kerr imprint.

Devoted to publishing controversial books that commercial publishers tend to avoid, the firm has shared the ups and downs of American radicalism. Because of Kerr's outspoken opposition to World War I, many of its publications were suppressed by the U.S. government under the notorious Espionage Act.

At the age of 138, the Kerr Company—a not-for-profit, worker-owned cooperative educational association—is not only a living link with the most vital radical traditions of the past, but also an organic part of today's struggles for peace and justice.

Unlike most other alternative publishers, the Kerr Company has never been subsidized by any political party, never had any "angels," never received any "grants." Our aim today remains what it always has been: to publish books that will help make this planet a good place to live!

As always, we need all the help we can get. If you would like to help the Charles H. Kerr Company, contact us today!

Publishers of Anti-Establishment Literature Since 1886
Charles H. Kerr Publishing Company
c h a r l e s h k e r r . c o m